G000096225

Learning from Experience

Learning from Experience

Perspectives on Poverty Reduction Strategies from Four Developing Countries

Edited by

David Peretz

Commonwealth Secretariat

Commonwealth Secretariat
Marlborough House
Pall Mall
London SW1Y 5HX
United Kingdom

Published by the Commonwealth Secretariat
Edited by Editors4Change Ltd
Designed by S.J.I. Services
Cover design by Tattersall Hammarling & Silk
Index by Indexing Specialists (UK) Ltd
Printed by Hobbs the Printers Ltd, Totton, Hampshire

Views and opinions expressed in this publication are the responsibility of the authors and should in no way be attributed to the institutions to which they are affiliated or to the Commonwealth Secretariat.

Wherever possible, the Commonwealth Secretariat uses paper sourced from sustainable forests or from sources that minimise a destructive impact on the environment.

Copies of this publication may be obtained from

The Publications Section
Commonwealth Secretariat
Marlborough House
Pall Mall
London SW1Y 5HX
United Kingdom
Tel: +44 (0)20 7747 6534
Fax: +44 (0)20 7839 9081
Email: publications@commonwealth.int
Web: www.thecommonwealth.org/publications

A catalogue record for this publication is available from the British Library.

ISBN: 978-0-85092-886-0 (paperback)
ISBN: 978-1-84859-012-0 (downloadable e-book)

Contents

Foreword

One of the key strengths of the Commonwealth is to bring together a diverse regional and cultural perspective on challenges that the membership is facing. This allows the sharing of lessons between nations and – where necessary – the promotion of change internationally. There is no greater or more important challenge facing either individual countries or the international community than reducing and eventually eliminating absolute poverty. This book is about the experience of four Commonwealth countries in the mechanics of meeting that challenge.

The way in which the international community engaged with the 'what' and 'how' of poverty reduction and development changed around the turn of the last century. The embodiment of this change was seen in two events. The first was the consensus on what was to be achieved, seen in the global commitment to the Millennium Development Goals (MDGs) by 2015 at the Millennium Summit in September 2000. The second was the consensus on how these goals should be achieved, which was set out at Monterrey in 2002. These have guided – albeit imperfectly – international efforts in this area ever since.

This progress was mirrored in the international financial institutions (IFIs). The language of structural adjustment and conditionality was abandoned for a new commitment to country ownership and partnership. The introduction of the Poverty Reduction Strategy Paper (PRSP) process in 1999 was emblematic of this new thinking. The stated aim was to create a comprehensive programme in which a country could articulate its priorities for poverty reduction and through which the international community could work to support those objectives.

Throughout the early years of the PRSP process, there was concern that this high aspiration was not being met in practice. There were multiple fears. First, that the content of PRSPs owed more to thinking in Washington than in countries themselves – a fear enhanced by the close association of PRSP design with eligibility for debt relief. Second, that consultation within governments and countries was limited. Third, was the fear that PRSPs were not being used effectively by donors, international institutions or governments. Finally, was the concern that a change of IFI language did not necessarily mean a change in mindset.

Since 1999, 18 Commonwealth countries have had at least one formal Poverty Reduction Strategy Paper. The purpose of this book is to draw on that accumulated experience to understand how the PRSP process has worked in practice and what its impact on policy – and consequently the lives of the people in these countries – has been. The four case studies get beneath the rhetoric of the process to provide insights for all those concerned with the practice of promoting poverty reduction. Appropriately, it emerges from the analysis that there is no single set of common lessons for the creation and use of PRSPs and no single blueprint.

Nonetheless, it is also clear that it is through this comparative work that the international community can continue the constant learning essential to achieving the central goal of prosperity for all.

Ransford Smith, Deputy Secretary-General of the Commonwealth

Acronyms

ADB	Asian Development Bank
ADP	Annual Development Plan (Bangladesh)
AGI	Association of Ghana Industries
APR	Annual progress report
ASDP	Agriculture Sector Development Programme (Tanzania)
BIDS	Bangladesh Institute of Development Studies
BWIs	Bretton Woods Institutions (IMF and World Bank)
CABS	Common Approach to Budget Support (group of donors)
CAS	Country-assistance strategy
CPESD	Co-ordinated Programme for Economic and Social Development (Ghana)
CPIA	Country Policy and Institutional Assessment (of the World Bank)
CSO	Civil society organisation
CSPGs	Cross-sectoral planning groups
CWIQ	Core Welfare Indicator Questionnaire (Ghana)
DEPD	Department of Economic Planning and Development (Malawi)
DFID	Department for International Development
DSCs	Development Support Credits
ERD	Economic Relations Division (Bangladesh)
FY	Fiscal year
GDP	Gross Domestic Product
GoT	Government of United Republic of Tanzania
GPRS	Ghana Poverty Reduction Strategy
GSS	Ghana Statistical Service
HIPC	Heavily indebted poor country
HNPSP	Health, Nutrition and Population Sector Programme (Bangladesh)
HPSP	Health and Population Sector Programme (Bangladesh)
I-PRSP	Interim Poverty Reduction Strategy Paper
ICPD	International Conference on Population and Development
IDA	International Development Association
IFI	International financial institutions
IMF	International Monetary Fund
IMG	Independent Monitoring Group
ISSER	Institute of Statistical, Social and Economic Research
JAS	Joint Assistance Strategy
JSA	Joint Staff Assessment (by IMF and World Bank)
JSAN	Joint Staff Advisory Note (by IMF and World Bank)
MCC	Millennium Challenge Corporation

MDAs	Ministries, departments and agencies
MDBS	Multi-Donor Budget Support (group of donors)
MDG	Millennium Development Goal
MEGS	Malawi Economic Growth Strategy
MEPD	Ministry of Economic Planning and Development (Malawi)
MGDS	Malawi Growth and Development Strategy
MoF	Ministry of Finance (Tanzania)
MoFEP	Ministry of Finance and Economic Planning (Ghana)
MPRS	Malawi Poverty Reduction Strategy
MPRSP	Malawi Poverty Reduction Strategy Paper
MTBF	Medium-term budget framework (Bangladesh)
MTEF	Medium-term expenditure framework
MTP	Medium-term priorities / medium-term programme (Ghana)
NCT	National Core Team (Malawi)
NDPC	National Development Planning Commission (Ghana)
NGO	Non-governmental organisation
NPES	National Poverty Eradication Strategy (Tanzania)
ODA	Official Development Assistance
OECD	Organisation for Economic Co-operation and Development
OECD DAC	OECD Development Assistance Committee
PAF	Performance assessment framework (agreed with the PRBS group)
PAF	Policy assessment framework
PEDP	Primary Education Development Programme (Tanzania)
PER	Public expenditure review (Tanzania)
PFMRP	Public Financial Management Reform Programme (Tanzania)
PLWHAS	People living with HIV/AIDS
PMS	Poverty Monitoring System (Tanzania)
PPEs	Pro-poor expenditures
PRBS	Poverty Reduction Budget Support
PRGF	Poverty Reduction and Growth Facility (of the IMF)
PRS	Poverty Reduction Strategy
PRSC	Poverty Reduction Support Credit
PRSP	Poverty Reduction Strategy Paper
PSRP	Public Sector Reform Programme
SAP	Structural Adjustment Programme
SMEs	Small and medium enterprises
SWAp	Sector-wide approach
TA	Technical assistance
TAS	Tanzania Assistance Strategy
TWG	Thematic Working Group (Malawi)
UNDP	United Nations Development Programme
VPO	Vice-President's Office

CHAPTER 1

Introduction

In recent times, there has been increasing recognition of the need to improve aid effectiveness through enhancing country ownership of reform programmes and better alignment of donor support behind effective country strategies. In the absence of such country ownership, the leverage of aid conditionality alone has often been found to be inadequate in bringing about sustained economic reforms. There is also a renewed emphasis on making aid more effective in reducing poverty, while at the same time promoting economic growth.

In response to these aid ideas, the World Bank and the IMF have adopted the 'Poverty Reduction Strategy' approach in providing development assistance to low-income countries. The PRS process involves the preparation of a Poverty Reduction Strategy Paper (PRSP) in order for a country to remain eligible for World Bank-IMF assistance – that is, concessional loans. The PRS/PRSP process is also increasingly being accepted as providing a basis for support from other international aid agencies and bilateral donors. In addition to promoting country ownership, the approach is expected to result in a lowering of transaction costs of delivering aid through a realignment and harmonisation of donor policies and practices[1].

Over the period 2004 to 2006 the Commonwealth Secretariat sponsored four studies to monitor implementation of the Poverty Reduction Strategy (PRS) process in Commonwealth countries. The purpose was to provide independent monitoring of how the PRS process, and support for it from international institutions, donors and others was working, as seen from the perspective of recipient countries. Each study was carried out jointly by a local research institution or consultant and a UK-based consultant. The four studies were:

- Monitoring Donor and IFI Support Behind Country-owned Poverty Reduction Strategies in The United Republic of Tanzania by Peretz and Wangwe (August 2004)
- Monitoring Donor and IFI Support Behind Country-owned Poverty Reduction Strategies in Ghana by Aryeetey and Peretz (August 2005)
- Monitoring Donor and IFI Support for Poverty Reduction Strategies: Malawi by Chipeta and Peretz (August 2006)
- Monitoring Donor Support to Poverty Reduction Strategy in Bangladesh: Rethinking the Rules of Engagement, which was prepared by Professor W Mahmud, with Dr B Mukherjee acting as Commonwealth Secretariat consultant (August 2006)

The studies were then discussed at successive annual meetings of the Commonwealth Finance Ministers in 2004, 2005 and 2006.

Events have moved on in all four countries since the studies were completed, and of course each country's circumstances are unique. Nonetheless, a number of common themes emerged from the research and these seem likely to continue to be relevant in the four countries and elsewhere. Issues emerging in Tanzania, which was one of the first countries to adopt a PRS, and in Ghana, where the initial PRS was launched in

2002, are likely to be the ones faced in other PRS countries in due course. In Malawi, the original PRS was also launched in 2002, but failures in macroeconomic policy and subsequent shortfalls in donor support meant it only began to be implemented effectively after a gap of several years, and rebuilding trust between government and development partners is a continuing process. In Bangladesh, the PRSP was launched towards the end of 2005. The following paragraphs discuss themes emerging from the studies under six headings: design of the strategy; the extent of country ownership, and how to strengthen it; implementation; accountability; alignment of development partner support; and improving donor practices and procedures and cutting transactions costs.

Overall picture

Design of Poverty Reduction Strategies

Countries have been learning from weaknesses in first generation Poverty Reduction Strategies and at the time of the studies, Tanzania, Ghana and Malawi were in the process of incorporating these lessons into their second-generation strategies. Key lessons include practicability, focus and ambition.

Practicability. What countries need as a basis both for their own policies and for external support is a comprehensive but practical medium-term national development strategy, defining an approach for all key aspects of development policy. 'Comprehensive' does not mean exhaustive or highly detailed; but the strategy does need to cover all the issues that are key to successful development and poverty reduction. 'Practical' means that the complexity, ambition and in some cases time frame of the strategy needs to match a country's ability to implement it. Particularly in countries where implementation capacity is relatively weak, it is important to identify a relatively limited set of achievable actions and expenditure priorities, which should be the strategy's focus. Indeed, in some cases it may be sensible to cost only those actions set out for the first year of the strategy, and rather than seeking to set out anything resembling a medium-term expenditure plan, simply illustrate a range of scenarios for later years.

Focus. Early PRSs, written in the first years of the century, tended to be focused excessively on policies and sectors that national officials thought to be of most interest to development partners, such as health, education and social protection – with less emphasis on other policies critical for development such as policies to enhance economic growth and create employment. This may partly explain the emergence or continuation in some countries of parallel national development strategies alongside the PRSs – in Tanzania a 'Medium-Term Plan for Growth and Poverty Reduction', in Ghana the 'Co-ordinated Programme for Economic and Social Development' and in Malawi the 'Malawi Economic Growth Strategy'. At the time of the studies, these parallel strategies were in the process of being integrated into second-generation PRSs, with much stronger emphases on economic growth and private-sector development – in some cases with a name change (in Malawi to the 'Malawi Growth and Development Strategy') to reflect the new, more comprehensive nature of the strategy. As discussed further below, some donors have been slow to adapt to this change of emphasis, preferring to focus on 'aid popular' interventions with a direct poverty focus rather than, for example, the investments in infrastructure and energy that are also essential for poverty reduction.

Ambition. A further lesson is that some of the early PRSs lacked ambition in the sense that they were based on IMF-agreed macroeconomic programmes that typically made conservative assumptions about possible aid flows and in some cases were difficult to adjust if aid flows turned out stronger than allowed for. Countries have been learning the advantages of illustrating more than one medium-term scenario, showing the faster progress that could be made with different levels or modalities of external assistance.

National ownership and how to strengthen it

The four studies reveal ownership to be a complex issue with many dimensions. There are issues of ownership among the key central ministries; ownership among a wider group of officials at national and local levels responsible for implementing the strategy; national ownership as endorsed by the elected government and parliament; ownership by stakeholders, such as the business sector and civil society; and ownership or at least a degree of understanding of the strategy among the general population. In countries eligible for heavily indebted poor country (HIPC) debt relief it appears that many of these dimensions of ownership were undermined initially by a widespread perception that the only reason for preparing Poverty Reduction Strategy Papers (PRSPs) was to qualify for debt relief, and that PRSPs had to be 'approved' by the boards of the International Monetary Fund (IMF) and World Bank in Washington. This is hardly surprising given the origin of the concept. Changes made in IMF and World Bank procedures after 2004 may have lessened this perception to some degree, and the studies suggest that ownership on most dimensions has strengthened over time – but in all four countries at the time of the studies, national ownership was far from complete. It is not proving easy to remove the perception that PRSs are primarily linked to the provision of external support, rather than being central national frameworks for growth and poverty reduction.

While the studies all find a high degree of ownership in the central departments – planning ministries or commissions (in Tanzania the Vice President's Office) and finance ministries – in many cases ownership and understanding of the strategy in implementing ministries was much less. Ownership and understanding among officials at the local level, including those with key implementation responsibilities, appeared to be even lower. The studies all suggest the need for greater efforts – not only to involve implementing ministries and local authorities more in strategy preparation, but also to ensure that they understand the strategy when it is agreed and ensure that it is implemented.

Parliaments had had little if any involvement with PRS processes at the time of the studies. In Tanzania in 2004, there appeared to be a widespread lack of awareness of the existence of the PRS among parliamentarians – an indication of how far there was to go to fully integrate the PRS into national processes. A common theme from the studies is the need for formal parliamentary scrutiny and endorsement of PRSs, as a symbol of true national ownership, and the role that civil society organisations (CSOs) and others could play in informing parliament and improving the quality of parliamentary debate.

CSOs were in all cases much involved in the process of developing initial PRS documents, and this has led to continuing involvement and some degree of ownership among the CSO community. In Malawi, for example, CSOs are putting much effort into spreading knowledge of the PRS among groups responsible for its implementation, parliamentarians and elsewhere. Business and private-sector representatives, by contrast, have felt much less involved, but were beginning to feel more involved in the preparation of second-generation PRSs with their stronger emphasis on growth and private-sector development.

A further common theme from the studies is the importance of outreach to the general population once a strategy is adopted, and the role that public accountability and monitoring, for example by CSOs, can play in implementation.

Implementation

The studies were concerned with the whole PRS process, including implementation, recognising that however well conceived or well written a strategy document is, it has little value unless it is implemented. Poor implementation was a key weakness, particularly in Malawi where the whole PRS process following the initial PRSP went badly off track. A number of common themes emerge from the studies, focused on different ways to improve financial management.

First among these is the need, ideally, for the strategy to be linked to a properly sequenced annual cycle of review of the PRS and its implementation, preparation of medium-term expenditure plans (usually in the form of medium-term expenditure frameworks – MTEFs), budget preparation, budget implementation and monitoring budget outturns. Where implementation capacity is weak, there needs to be at least a firm link between the strategy and annual budget preparation.

Second, is the important and continuing role that finance ministries can play, in co-operation with planning ministries/commissions, in ensuring that annual departmental budgets are clearly and transparently linked to the strategy. This requires effective arrangements for challenging ministries' budget bids and for monitoring and evaluating outturns to ensure that plans when agreed are executed effectively.

Moving to national accountability

A further theme of the studies is the importance of developing and strengthening systems of domestic accountability. Over the years, development partners have established quite elaborate arrangements for ensuring accountability to themselves for governments' development strategies and progress made in implementing policies and projects. Arrangements for continuing policy dialogue with budget support groups of donors, and also at the sector level, have acted to strengthen such accountability to donors further. To avoid undermining moves to strengthen national accountability, development partners, including the international financial institutions (IFIs), need over time to draw back from these arrangements, while governments need to strengthen their own arrangements for accounting to parliament and people for the country's development strategy and its implementation.

In particular, governments should move to developing and presenting to parliament the policy contents of IMF letters of intent, like PRS documents, as their own policy statements. (For the IMF, the government could then simply send a covering letter enclosing the government's policy document). Similarly, where policy assessment frameworks (PAFs) are developed in co-operation with development partners, these should be treated and presented as government statements of policy intentions, with the government, not donors, responsible for monitoring and reporting progress on its commitments.

These and other improvements in governance require domestic political commitment; without that, donor support for the institutions of governance and accountability will not be effective.

Donor alignment

From the outset of the PRS approach, and most explicitly in commitments made in the Paris Declaration on Aid Effectiveness in 2005, donors have agreed that where a country has a viable PRS in place, then external aid will be aligned with country priorities as set out in that strategy. The studies – and subsequent discussions among Commonwealth Finance Ministers suggesting similar experiences in other countries – throw much light on what progress is being made in practice on these commitments and what more needs to be done. It is a process likely to take some time, involving as it does reconciling systems and priorities of individual donors with those of country governments.

One highly positive development has been the shift away from support for individual projects, each requiring separate negotiation and not always within the government's priorities, and towards general budget support and support for sector strategies through basket-funding arrangements. The studies suggest that in the past, aid provided for individual projects has not only sometimes been in conflict with national priorities, but also has not been captured properly in government financial and other statistics, undermining the country's financial and resource allocation systems. Some donors have preferred to bypass the government and channel aid through non-governmental organisations (NGOs). Moreover, in some countries projects have in the past been subject to frequent cancellations, particularly where projects were inadequately informed by local knowledge of what works and what does not, leaving a substantial proportion of committed aid unutilised.

There is, however, some way to go to achieve a situation where development partners simply accept the government's priorities as set out in the PRS and sector strategies and support them. Both budget and sector support are still subject to separate negotiated conditions. As suggested above, it would seem preferable for these policy commitments to be presented for what they are – more specific government commitments made within the framework of the PRS for which the government holds itself accountable in the first instance to its parliament and people.

Where confidence among development partners is weak, it may be more realistic to seek to establish arrangements where donors can channel funds into sector baskets – sector-wide approaches (SWAps) – rather than expecting a rapid move towards a more substantial measure of direct budget support.

Where funding for sector baskets or individual projects continues, it will be important to ensure that it falls within overall government priorities, and as far as possible is accounted for within government systems. This applies also to aid delivered through NGOs, where it is important to develop the NGO/government partnership: donors should not be seeking to deliver aid through NGOs as a way of circumventing government. Where support for a project or sector does not fall within government priorities, on occasion governments should be prepared to say 'no'.

Improving other donor practices and procedures

The Paris Declaration contains many other commitments to improve donor practices and procedures and aid modalities, to reduce transactions costs for recipients and improve aid effectiveness – for example, using country systems where possible. However, progress in implementing these commitments at the country level remains slow – perhaps in some cases reflecting stronger ownership of the Paris principles by agency policy staff at headquarters than by staff operating on the ground.

One issue for recipients is a concern that despite its other advantages, budget financing could prove less stable and predictable than project finance. In particular, there is seen by many to be a risk that budget-support donors could suspend the totality of their budget support because of relatively modest policy disagreements or political events. Some donors are showing the way by making firm long-term commitments for at least substantial parts of their budget support.

Another issue is the continuing large numbers of inward donor visiting missions, which place high demands both on government and development partners. Where missions are technical, they can of course add value. The problem arises when – as is too often the case – they provide little technical added value, but tie up the scarce time of senior officials. Increasingly elaborate systems of local consultation machinery add further demands on the time of the same officials. The best approach – being pioneered by some of the countries that were studied – is probably to cut back visiting missions to an absolute minimum, to try to focus more on local consultation and to set a clear annual timetable for joint consultations with all budget donors and IFIs.

Despite improvements in government financial management and accounting systems, these are still being used too little by donors, reflecting agency rules or operational habits that should be changed.

A closer local-development partnership of the kind that is being developed in all four countries will require other changes from development partners. All significant partners need to organise themselves locally so they can engage effectively in policy discussion in-country. In some cases this may require more local staff, but more importantly it will require empowerment of local staff by head offices to take decisions locally; better arrangements for continuity when local staff rotate; and implementation of arrangements for specialisation among development partners, assigning different donors or agencies the acknowledged lead in different sectors or policy issues.

In too many cases, donor co-ordination is still being driven by donors rather than by recipient governments. The early experience in Tanzania, which is drawn on elsewhere, suggests that strong government leadership can do much to progress implementation in each country of the global commitments that have been made to align donor support behind country strategies, and to co-ordinate and harmonise donor practices and procedures to reduce the administrative burden on government. Such strong leadership is also usually welcome by donors. In addition, in too many cases, monitoring and evaluation of progress on this agenda – essentially implementation of the Paris Declaration on Aid Effectiveness – is being carried out by donors. The Tanzanian experience points to the potential value in all countries of setting up arrangements for truly independent monitoring of such progress.

Concluding comment

One final lesson that emerges from the four reports (presented in chapters 2–5, below) and subsequent discussions at meetings of Commonwealth Finance Ministers is the potential value to countries from being able to learn from each other's experiences in developing and implementing Poverty Reduction Strategies. It is hoped that the four studies will encourage further interaction between countries facing similar issues in implementing a PRS approach and handling their relationships with development partners.

Note

1. The new aid consensus was embodied in the Paris Declaration of March 2005, which was a follow-up to the Rome Declaration of 2003.

CHAPTER 2

Monitoring Donor and IFI Support Behind Country-owned Poverty Reduction Strategies in the United Republic of Tanzania

David Peretz and Professor Samuel Wangwe

I Introduction

This chapter presents the first in the series of country reports prepared under the Commonwealth Secretariat project to monitor implementation of the Poverty Reduction Strategy (PRS) process in Commonwealth countries. This report on the United Republic of Tanzania was prepared jointly by David Peretz, an independent senior consultant to the Commonwealth Secretariat, and Professor Samuel Wangwe of the Economic and Social Research Foundation, Dar es Salaam, Tanzania. It was completed in August 2004.

In preparing the report, we drew extensively on previous evaluations of the Tanzanian experience, notably the 2002 report of the Independent Monitoring Group and the more recent 2004 evaluation carried out jointly by the International Monetary Fund's (IMF) Independent Evaluation Office and the World Bank's Operations Evaluation Department. We held a series of discussions in Tanzania with representatives of government, the private sector, civil society and development partners, including a workshop to discuss the initial findings, and a second series of discussions based on a draft of the report. We also discussed our findings with officials of the IMF and World Bank in Washington, DC. The conclusions, however, are our own.

The report and findings of this chapter focus on a set of key issues that were intended to serve as a template for the other country reports produced under this project. Given Tanzania's relatively extended experience with the Poverty Reduction Strategy Paper (PRSP) process, we have focused as much on areas where others can learn from that country's experience as on areas for attention in Tanzania itself. Even in Tanzania, which at the time of the report had more than three years' experience of implementation, it was too early to say much about final outcomes and results. The focus of this report, therefore, is more on processes and intermediate outcomes.

The chapter is organised as follows. Section II describes the PRS process as it evolved and continues to evolve in Tanzania. Section III examines issues to do with the strategy itself and its implementation. Section IV discusses the quality of support being given by development partners. Finally, Section V gives a summary of our key findings, including suggestions about areas for attention in Tanzania and possible lessons for other countries and the international community.

II Evolution of the PRS process in Tanzania

Origins of the Tanzanian PRS

The first PRS for the United Republic of Tanzania was prepared in 2000, primarily as a response to the HIPC (heavily indebted poor country) initiative. However, it followed a process of national-strategy formulation that had been under way for some years. The Development Vision 2025 document, published in 1998, set out a vision of development up to 2025. The National Poverty Eradication Strategy (NPES), published in 1997, was more specific about strategies and policies, and development of the PRS and the initial PRS paper coincided with, and took the place of, an exercise to develop a national action plan for implementation of the NPES. Also of relevance was the Tanzania Assistance Strategy (TAS), which was being drafted together with development partners at the time the PRS was being developed, and the public expenditure review (PER) process, which by 1998 had become a main vehicle for policy formulation linked to the medium-term expenditure framework (MTEF) and involving development partners as well as government.

Thus, in implementing the PRS process, the government was able to build on these pre-existing exercises. The PRSP superseded – in a sense became – the action plan for implementing the NPES. Very much in the spirit of the PRS initiative, it was designed to serve both as a document for the Bretton Woods Institutions (BWIs; required both for HIPC debt relief and continued concessional assistance) and as a national action plan for co-ordination of government policies aimed at poverty reduction. Because of the HIPC timetable, the PRSP was produced with some speed. The consultation process, while extensive, was felt by many to have been truncated. At the same time, the selected priorities – with a heavy emphasis on health and education spending alongside macro-

---

Box 2.1: Key features of Tanzania's 2000 PRSP

The 2000 PRSP identified the following three broad areas and set out government priorities, targets and benchmarks in each:
- reduction of income poverty;
- improving human capabilities, survival and social wellbeing; and
- containing extreme vulnerability.

It required sector policies and strategies to adhere to the national development agenda of eradicating absolute poverty, and to address the identified policy objectives and targets.

The PRSP also directed financial resources (government budget and donor support) to the priority sectors and areas. The priority sectors listed in the original PRSP included agriculture, basic education, primary health care, water and sanitation, rural roads, the legal and judicial system and HIV/AIDS. In addition, the PRSP identified priority cross-cutting issues, which included gender equality, preservation of the natural environment and employment creation.

The PRSP called for an effective poverty monitoring system and identified indicators (mostly outcome and impact indicators) to be used in tracking progress. The current list has 60 indicators in the following 12 categories: income poverty; roads; agriculture; education; health; water and sanitation; survival; nutrition; governance; gender; poverty–environment linkage; and vulnerability.

The PRSP is updated annually in a progress report, and at the time of the country report was undergoing a more comprehensive review, three years after the original PRSP.

---

economic policy – also probably owed something to perceptions of what was required for HIPC relief. Successive PRSP updates have in effect broadened priorities to give more emphasis, for example, to policies to support private-sector development and invest in infrastructure.

Integration of the PRS into Tanzania's national policy-making framework

Tanzania's PRSP has developed from its original form, but at the time of writing still had some way to go before being fully established as **the** national framework guiding all policies and initiatives aimed at growth and poverty reduction, driving sector policies and strategies, linked with the budget through the PER/MTEF, and setting targets with progress monitored through the Poverty Monitoring System (PMS). It is still seen by many as a strategy driven by external partners; and by many within government as of limited relevance to their ministries. Meanwhile, the endorsement by Tanzania's cabinet and publication of a separate medium-term strategy for growth and poverty reduction, prepared by the President's Office (Planning and Privatisation division) was a confusing factor. Moreover, despite arrangements for co-ordinating PRS formulation and implementation across government (see box 2.2), the process of integrating the PRS with parallel policy frameworks was still under way and by no means complete at the time of the Tanzanian study.

Most of the priority sectors have developed sector strategies and programmes based on their sector policies, which specifically mention the Vision 2025 and the NPES as their guiding framework. In addition, most ministries have developed strategic plans (in essence, action plans with monitorable indicators) based on sector strategies in the context of the Public Sector Reform Programme (PSRP) under the guidance of the Public Service Management Central Establishment. At the local government level, there is the Local Government Reform Programme (LGRP), which had started in 38 councils at the time of writing. The aim of the LGRP is to get similar results to those aimed for at the national level – that is, action plans set in a results-based management system.

Box 2.2: PRS co-ordinating arrangements and responsibilities

The PRS process in Tanzania is co-ordinated by the Poverty Reduction Strategy Technical Committee under the guidance of a committee of ministers. This committee draws members (typically directors of planning) from the PRS priority sectors, including Ministry of Finance (MoF), Vice-President's Office (VPO), Ministry of Agriculture and Food Security, Ministry of Education and Culture, Ministry of Health, Ministry of Water and Livestock Development, Ministry of Community Development, Gender and Children, Prime Minister's Office, President's Office (Planning and Privatisation), President's Office (Regional Administration and Local Government), Ministry of Works, Tanzania Association of NGOs (TANGO), Bank of Tanzania and co-opted members depending on the subject being discussed. The chair of the PRS Technical Committee is the deputy permanent secretary, Ministry of Finance, and the secretariat is provided by the Poverty Eradication Division – Vice-President's Office.

The PRS is thus in practice led by both the MoF and VPO. The work of the Technical Committee involves follow-up on implementation, preparation of annual progress reports and reporting to the PMS Steering Committee and to the Committee of Ministers, as well as to development partners.

Box 2.3: Sector reform programmes supported by basket finance

- The Primary Education Development Programme (PEDP), Health Sector Programme, Local Government Reform Programme, Public Expenditure Review and Poverty Monitoring Master Plan (PMMP) are all well established.
- Basket funding arrangements were launched in 2004 for the Public Sector Reform Programme and Business Environment Strengthening in Tanzania (BEST).
- As of 2004, proposals were at an advanced stage to create new baskets to support the Public Financial Management Reform Programme (PFMRP) and Agriculture Sector Development Programme (ASDP).

In parallel with these sector strategies and alongside its involvement with PRS preparation and monitoring, the Ministry of Finance since 1998 has continued to lead the Public Finance Reform Programme, which led to the annual PER and MTEF – the twin processes that guide the national budget. Separately, the MoF also leads the TAS initiative, designed to provide government guidance and leadership in co-ordination of donor support; and is the main interlocutor for discussions with the IMF on policies supported by the Poverty Reduction and Growth Facility (PRGF), and with the World Bank and Poverty Reduction Budget Support (PRBS) group of donors in discussions of policies supported by the PRBS group and the Bank's Poverty Reduction Support Credit (PRSC).

Although these various processes commenced at different times and are co-ordinated by different ministries and institutions, they are all linked. However, not all ministries see and appreciate the linkages. Even where the linkages are seen and appreciated, it is not always obvious how to tie the processes together in practice. Different government ministries and institutions have, therefore, tended to continue to focus on their own respective initiatives, and to treat the PRS as a mandate of the MoF and VPO. The one central link that does tie most activities together in Tanzania is the annual process of budget decisions (see box 2.4). There are also still some disconnects between MTEF/ PER processes, budget decisions and the PRS – both in substance and timing – although the government is working to rationalise all these processes within the National Budget and PRS frameworks.

Policy conditionality set by donors and the BWIs

As noted above, alongside the national processes, the MoF continues to have separate discussions with the IMF about support from the PRGF, and with the World Bank and

Box 2.4: Annual budget process

- **Budget guidelines** issued in January: a three-year rolling medium-term expenditure plan put together by the Budget Guidelines Committee
- **The MTEF/PER** process concluded in April/May comprises a macro-fiscal framework and detailed MTEFs incorporating PRS priorities for priority sectors
- **The annual budget**, submitted to parliament by mid-June
- **The PRSP Progress Report**, scheduled for publication around November (but in practice there have been significant delays)

Learning from Experience

PRBS group of donors about their support under the PRSC and bilateral budget support arrangements. These discussions result in negotiated documents, which specify actions to be undertaken, outputs expected and benchmarks for continued budget support. For the PRGF, the Government of Tanzania had up to the time of writing continued to prepare a letter of intent signed by the Minister of Finance stipulating commitments to adhere to sound macroeconomic management, and making projections of the macro-economic variables and setting structural benchmarks. For the PRBS and PRSC, there is a performance assessment framework (PAF), which lists actions and outputs to be achieved by specified dates to warrant continued budget support. Currently, it is a joint PAF (for both PRSC and PRBS) with a list of prior actions and triggers for subsequent disbursements. Preparation of the PAF matrix and updating is co-ordinated by the Ministry of Finance and involves both central and sector ministries.

Donor co-ordination, the Tanzania Assistance Strategy and work of the Independent Monitoring Group

The co-operation between donors in the PRBS group reflects a growing willingness on the part of donors to harmonise and align their support for government actions and policies using either the budget process or by providing support for sectoral investment programmes through basket funding (see box 2.3, above). The 2002 Rome declaration on aid alignment and harmonisation gave impetus to this process, which is probably as far advanced in Tanzania as in any other developing country. The government is using the Tanzania Assistance Strategy (TAS) process to reinforce this development, and the 2002 report of the Independent Monitoring Group (IMG; see annex for a summary) also helped.

The Implementation Action Plan for the TAS (June 2003) identifies four priorities:
- **Improving predictability of aid flows.** There have been some improvements, including shared projections, changes to the nature of conditionality and earlier disbursement within the fiscal year, but important challenges remain.
- **Integrating donor funds into the government budget.** Some partners have re-sponded to improvements in the government's financial management system by agreeing to channel a higher proportion of aid through budget support and bas-ket funding, but capturing in the budget donor resources channelled direct to projects remains a challenge. Few donors have as yet agreed to use the new mechanism to channel such resources through the budget (see box 2.5, below).
- **Rationalising and harmonising processes.** The government bears a double bur-den: of a very extensive system of consultation and other co-ordination mecha-nisms with locally based development partners; and a continued burden of donor missions from capitals and head offices requiring time of senior officials (the Ministry of Finance estimates there were more than 500 such missions in 2002/03). Some progress has been made in establishing 'quiet times' of the year, and in promoting joint reviews and missions (as in the PRSC/PRBS group), but much remains to be done.
- **Capacity building** for aid co-ordination and external resource management, to help strengthen the government's leadership role in these areas.

Box 2.5: Integrating donor funds into the government budget

Increasing the proportion of aid flows captured in the government's budget – both budget estimates and disbursements – is an agreed objective under the TAS. It hinges on success in ongoing reforms of the government's public financial management system. Important elements include the Integrated Financial Management System (IFMS), the PER/MTEF framework, the Public Finance and Public Procurement Acts 2001, and implementation of the Public Financial Management Reform Programme. The IFMS, which began to be rolled out in 1998, provides a single computerised payments system for the government, providing full financial control and reporting.

Development partners have responded to these improvements with some increase in funds channelled through the budget, notably budget support and basket funding – which increased from around 30 per cent of all aid flows in 2002 to around 40 per cent in 2004.

The remaining challenge is to capture funds that flow directly to projects being implemented by sector ministries and local government. Around 650 separate projects were being implemented in fiscal year (FY) 2002/03. The Accountant-General has created a mechanism for donors to channel funds to projects through the government's accounts, a mechanism that can even be used for disbursements to non-governmental organisation (NGO) and private-sector projects. As of 2004, despite considerable efforts made by the Accountant-General's department, only a few donors had begun to make use of this mechanism. Officials from Canada (which had to pass domestic legislation to make this possible), the UK, Norway, Ireland and the United Nations Development Programme (UNDP) all attended training sessions with the Accountant-General's department. However, as of November 2003 only four development partners had indicated readiness to use the new mechanism.

At the time of the Tanzanian study, the government was considering an early review of the TAS with a view to strengthening it. In parallel, development partners in Tanzania were beginning to discuss the possible development of a Joint Assistance Strategy (JAS) – covering such issues as aid modalities, ways to improve predictability and ways to reduce inward missions and other development partner demands on government – recognising that any such strategy would need in due course to be merged into a new TAS.

The PRS review

At the time of writing, the Vice-President's Office was leading the process of producing a new PRS. There had already been a first round of consultations – including with parliamentarians and the private sector, as well as civil society organisations (CSOs) and development partners, and work was just starting on the first full draft. Two further rounds of consultations were planned on the first and second drafts, before the adoption of the strategy. We discuss many of the issues that arose in section III, below.

Outcomes to 2004

According to BWI and government figures, the PRS process has been associated with a substantial increase in external financial support for the Tanzanian government, with external flows rising from 25 per cent of budget spending in 1998 to over 40 per cent in

2003 (see table 2.1). Over the same period, the proportion of gross aid flows provided in programme (including debt relief) rather than project aid increased from 40 per cent to 60 per cent. On the other hand, figures from donors published by the OECD Development Assistance Committee (DAC) suggest that expressed as a proportion of GDP, total aid flows to Tanzania have been relatively flat over the last decade, running at around 13 per cent of GDP (see table 2.2). So at least part of the recorded increase in flows to government may reflect a diversion of aid previously channelled to NGOs, or provided in the form of time of foreign consultants, and part may reflect a capturing of flows not previously recorded in the government's budget – in many ways welcome developments in themselves.

As of 2004, it was still thought to be too soon to expect to see any substantial results of the 2000 PRS and its implementation for growth and poverty reduction. However, as table 2.3 illustrates, growth had picked up since 2000, and although there was a downturn in 2003, this was less than might have been expected given adverse weather and other conditions.

Table 2.1: External assistance to the Government of Tanzania
Grants and net loans, including HIPC debt relief

	FY1998	FY2000	FY2002	FY2003	FY2004 (proj)
% GDP	4.0	6.0	5.9	8.6	9.7
% Government expenditure	25.5	34.5	33.5	41.3	40.9
Programme aid as % of grants and loans (gross)	39.2	35.8	58.2	56.7	60.7

Sources: World Bank, IMF, Government of Tanzania

Table 2.2: Official development assistance (ODA)
Disbursements, $m

	1996	1998	2000	2002
ODA, nominal	877	1,000	1,022	1,233
ODA, real	729	910	978	1,164
ODA as % of GDP	13.5	12.0	11.3	13.1

Sources: OECD DAC, IMF, World Bank

Table 2.3: Real GDP growth (%)

1996	1997	1998	1999	2000	2001	2002	2003
4.2	3.3	4.0	4.7	4.9	5.7	6.2	5.6

Source: Government of Tanzania

III Quality of the PRS and its implementation

This section seeks to answer a set of key questions about the nature and quality of the Tanzanian Poverty Reduction Strategy process. Here we focus on the whole process – including PRSP documents, the process of drawing them up and strategy implementation, including the link with budget and other government processes – not just on the PRSP documents themselves.

Ownership

A central question is how far the PRS is seen and accepted in the United Republic of Tanzania as a country-owned and country-driven strategy – by the government, parliament and other country stakeholders; or is it seen as just another requirement for qualifying for external assistance?

While the PRS was developed through a broad-based participatory process, **it seems to be widely accepted that the depth of ownership of the initial PRS adopted in 2000 was not great**, although it was certainly seen and accepted by the cabinet as a government strategy. As already noted, the strategy was prepared in haste, to obtain HIPC debt relief, with both the process and content designed to follow a Washington 'template'. The content also focused on increased social expenditures, in a manner thought to be a requirement for HIPC relief. Nevertheless, the strategy did benefit from an extensive consultation and participation process, and also from pre-existing longer-term national strategies – Vision 2025 and the National Poverty Eradication Strategy – to which it was closely linked.

Ownership has grown and is still growing, through a series of annual progress reports and implementation. There is strong ownership at the top of the key central ministries – the Ministry of Finance and the Vice-President's Office. At the same time, there has been continued and broad engagement with other stakeholders including civil society through working groups, national debates, the organisation of 'poverty weeks' and so on. 'Ownership' is a complex concept, however, and best discussed in terms of individual components, and in relation to the whole PRS 'process' rather than the strategy document itself. At the time of the study, **there were clearly still many weak links**. There was also **a continuing widely shared perception that it was a strategy prepared more for external partners than for internal partners**, and that it did not feature as frequently in high-level policy statements as it would if it were the guiding domestic strategy. The publication in 2004 of a separate medium-term plan for growth and poverty reduction was also confusing.

Ownership within government

As was recognised in the government's guide for the 2003/04 review of the PRS, 'there is still a lack of awareness and ownership of the PRS across all levels and sectors of government'. Recognition of the importance of the PRS is especially weak at the local level, and among sector ministries other than those that were original PRS priority areas – health and education. As noted earlier, sectors focus on their sector strategies, which are based on Vision 2025, the NPES and the PRS and TAS, but do not necessarily realise they are implementing the PRS. Members of the PRS Technical Committee from different ministries have tended to operate more in their individual capacities, rather than as effective representatives of their institutions. Hence **many ministries continue to view the PRS process as primarily the mandate of the VPO, so that even those who are actively implementing the components of the PRS are often unaware that they are doing so – and in some cases are unaware of the existence of the PRS.**

This matters, because implementation depends on the efforts of sector ministries and local and district government, and depends in particular on these units integrating the strategy fully into their normal decision-making processes. As is discussed further below, a key measure of 'ownership' is the extent to which the PRS is integrated into normal government decision-making processes, and implemented in a way that delivers the strategy's objectives.

Engagement of civil society, parliament and other stakeholders

How do other domestic partners – notably representatives of civil society, the private sector and parliament – view the Poverty Reduction Strategy process? Civil society organisations, and particularly the NGOs that were actively involved in the fight for debt relief, were involved in the preparation of the original PRSP, and continue to be involved in the Poverty Monitoring System (in the steering committee and in the Technical Working Groups) and the poverty policy week. NGOs working together in the NGO policy forum made a substantial and impressive written contribution to the PRS review. The private sector's involvement remained minimal, however. Members of parliament also generally remained out of the loop, except for a few workshops that were organised to inform them about the PRSP and progress reports. (Key PRSP documents are also shared with MPs for their information.)

Up until 2003/2004, the virtual absence of parliamentary interest in the process was particularly striking. In a parliamentary system as in Tanzania, parliament might be expected to play a much larger role in developing the PRS than it did – perhaps through the Finance and Economic Affairs Committee. As it was, **the lack of awareness of the PRS among parliamentarians was an indication of how far there was to go to fully integrate the PRS into national processes.** True national 'ownership' of the process would and should be reflected in increased accountability to the people, and unless MPs become more involved, there must be doubts about the political sustainability of the process.

The PRS review guide recognised the need to further foster country ownership 'by improving participation ... [and to] develop a PRS communications strategy to raise public awareness of the PRS', and to strengthen the participation of democratic institutions such as local councils and parliament 'to create a genuine country ownership'. **So it is encouraging that an active process of consultation on what was to become the 2005 PRS was launched with parliamentarians and the chairs of the key parliamentary committees.** The country report of that year recommends that, 'Ways should be found also to allow parliament to engage regularly in the process of annual PRS review, perhaps by including the PRSP progress report among budget documents, so it can be scrutinised during budget debates. It will be important at the local level to achieve greater awareness of the process and involvement of local councillors, who are responsible for the local development machinery'.

The country report also highlights that: 'It will be important in the PRS review [of 2003/04] to allow much more time than in the original PRS process for in-depth consultations with civil society and other stakeholders. And in particular the quality of consultation and discussion of macro-policy issues needs to be improved'. In fact, over the PRS period the macro framework has been adapted and improved, at least in part as a result of input from independent outsiders. Nevertheless, many still feel excluded from the debate on this central aspect of policy. The technical nature of some of the macro-policy issues should not be seen as a reason for limiting debate, but rather as a challenge to those concerned – in government and in the IMF – to frame issues in a way that makes them accessible and understandable to non-experts. We do not believe this is an impossible task. This is relevant to the continuous process of consultation inherent in the PRS process, including at the time of regular reviews under the PRGF arrangement, as well as to the process of producing a new PRSP. Some discussion already takes place at the annual PER review meetings, and thought might be given to developing other suitable fora for discussion.

A national framework or a basis for accountability to development partners?

Underlying many of the issues discussed above is the question: is the PRS primarily a national framework for guiding policy action, or is it first and foremost an instrument of accountability to the BWIs and other development partners? There is no doubt that as originally conceived in Washington, PRSPs were intended to be the former. **It is also clear that many of the Washington-based processes surrounding the PRS, with the PRSP apparently needing to be 'approved' by the BWI boards, give an impression that it is the latter. It will take a determined effort to dispel this impression.**

In Tanzania, the PRS is serving as a national process for policy dialogue and identification of priorities for more effective growth and poverty-reduction policies, with annual updates through the PRS progress reports and with the annual poverty policy weeks providing a forum for exchange of ideas among the stakeholders. While, as noted in section II, the strategy was not yet fully integrated into national policy-making arrangements at the time of the study, the PRS was increasingly being considered by the government and civil society, as well as external development partners, to be the national framework that guides policy and actions for growth and poverty reduction. At the same time, PRSP documents are subject to 'assessment' by the BWIs, and scrutiny and 'endorsement' by their boards, and are often produced to meet Washington timetables. PRSPs and progress reports also provide indicators and benchmarks that external partners use to judge progress and as triggers for assistance.

Our view is that a national policy document, once approved, should not be subjected to external approvals by the BWIs, or any other external partners. Obviously the BWIs and other external partners have to make their own decisions about how much support to give, but it is important to avoid giving the impression that the PRS needs BWI 'approval'. **This may require changes in BWI procedures, which in any event should focus more on assessing the whole PRS process, including implementation arrangements, and much less on the quality of individual documents.**

In parallel, and linked to this change, the 2004 study found that it was **important to strengthen the Tanzanian government's domestic accountability for the strategy and its implementation.** It is not just that parliament needs to be more involved, as was planned, but parliament also needs the resources, procedures and time to become an effective form of accountability. Moreover, PRS, budget and related documents should not just be published, but publicised, put on websites, with channels provided for comment.

There were other actions that could help establish the PRS as the guiding national policy framework in the country:

- **More frequent, high-level policy statements giving it this status**
- **Clarification that the 2004 PRS would encompass the recently published medium-term plan for growth and poverty reduction, and that they are not rival strategies**
- **Adopting a new national name for the strategy, dropping the BWI nomenclature**

With the PRS becoming more clearly a national document and process, some argue the case for negotiating a separate 'contract' between the government and development partners, perhaps building on the existing PAF agreed with the World Bank and PRBS group of donors, and the letter of intent to the IMF. Our own view is that would be a mistake. It would undermine ownership, and could lead to a return to old-style conditionality. The better approach, more consistent with the underlying PRS philosophy, is to accept that in a country like Tanzania, with over 40 per cent of the budget (including 20 per cent of recurrent expenditure) financed by support from donors and external agencies, any central government growth and poverty reduction strategy is bound to serve a dual purpose: to act as the government's own strategy, and to form the basis of an accountability contract with donors. PRSPs are indeed intended to play this dual role – in the words of the Bank/Fund guidance on good practices: 'PRSPs aim to serve as the framework for both domestic policies and programmes to reduce poverty, as well as for development aid'. There will inevitably be a degree of tension between country ownership and the requirement for acceptance by the BWIs and donors as a strategy deserving their support, including particular benchmarks and actions to which they attach importance. The question is: how is this tension being addressed, and could it be handled better? There are both many positive developments in this respect in Tanzania, and scope for further improvements, as discussed further below.

Nature and quality of the PRS

What is the nature of the Poverty Reduction Strategy in Tanzania? What improvements had to be made up until 2004, and what further improvements should be made in future?

Broad or narrow?

A central question here is: is it/should it be a strategy narrowly focused on direct poverty reducing interventions and macro stability; or is it/should it be something closer to a national development strategy, encompassing all elements of policy and spending related to economic growth and poverty reduction? While the PRS started as something close to the former – seen to be a requirement for HIPC debt relief – it has steadily developed into a broader and more comprehensive strategy, and **the PRS review of 2003/04 seemed set to and should mark a further step change in the same direction, turning the PRS process into more of a comprehensive development strategy for growth**

and poverty reduction, one that drives other strategies. At the time of writing, we understood the government was considering a new name for the strategy, as suggested above, which would help signal this change.

While it is important not to lose the progress made in focusing more attention on key social investments in health, education, water and establishing a poverty monitoring system, this widening of scope would (we believe) be an altogether welcome development. First, the sectors and cross-cutting issues that were being added are crucial for sustainable poverty reduction: policies and expenditures that create jobs, support livelihoods, address underlying problems of industrial competitiveness and improve the environment for private-sector development, assist agriculture, strengthen infrastructure, address issues in energy supply and mining, and improve security and policing. Second, a more comprehensive national development strategy may be easier to fully integrate into the day-to-day running of government, with all ministries involved, something that is crucial for effective implementation. Third, although this may not have been fully recognised, **the shift to a broader strategy is to some degree implicit in the decision already made to make the new PRS more results based.** So, for example, a focus on increasing school attendance automatically points to the need for better transport or provision of nutrition at schools, as well as better school buildings and teachers.

This does not mean sacrificing priority setting. It will be even more important for a more comprehensive document to specify the main priorities for the period of the strategy. However, priorities should be set recognising that policy actions and expenditures in non-priority sectors remain important and complement actions in priority sectors. The changes may even involve reorientation of non-priority sectors to complement better the priority sectors. Moreover, the strategy needs to go beyond setting priorities for public expenditures. It is equally important to identify priorities for changes in policy – for example, the need to adopt policies designed to support private-sector development by reducing unnecessary bureaucracy and removing an array of obstacles that raise the cost of doing business. Such policy changes may carry no budget cost, but may be as important for growth and poverty reduction as decisions about the allocation of public resources.

Bottom up or top down?

Another issue is how far the PRS should become a bottom-up rather than top-down process. As individual sector strategies develop and mature, it probably will/should become more bottom up, starting from local government and the community level, as well as sector strategies and incorporating these in the overall national strategy. A central feature of the 2004 PRS was likely to be a matrix relating desired outcomes to specific-sector actions. This is linked with the issue we discuss elsewhere of integrating the PRS process better with other parallel policy-making and implementing processes in government. **Those making the sector contributions – normally directors of policy and planning – and those making community/ local development contributions such as councillors and local officials should see defining and adapting the PRS as central to their own strategies, action plans and decision-taking, rather than as separate, additional processes.**

Risk analysis

The study for Tanzania found that the 2004 PRS might also usefully discuss some of the risks that could derail the strategy, such as HIV/AIDS, and what actions could be taken to mitigate or respond to such risks.

How well was the strategy being implemented?

There is a growing awareness both in government and among development partners that however good the strategy document is, and however well conducted the preparation process, it is worthless unless it is implemented effectively. This recognition that it is the whole PRS 'process' that matters much more than the PRSP itself (however well written) is itself a welcome development. The process encompasses or should encompass links with sector strategies and action plans and the annual budget process, and also implementation and results achieved on the ground.

Integration with mainstream policy formation and implementation

At the time of writing, there was only limited information about final outcomes achieved on the ground in Tanzania, and our main focus was on the intermediate stages – in particular the links between the PRS and government decision-making processes. The discussion above describes progress made to 2004 in integrating the PRS process into the national policy-making and implementation framework. Disconnects still exist between the PRS, sectoral strategies and action plans, PERs and the MTEF and budget decision-making. **Yet a successful PRS process requires all these processes to be well linked together and all those concerned with its implementation to see the strategy as an integral part of the work of their ministries and institutions**, not as a separate activity for which responsibility lies in the VPO or MoF. **In particular, a much firmer link between the PRS, sector strategies and budget decisions is needed**. This was recognised in the Ministry of Finance, which in 2004 was working to rationalise all the processes within the national budget and PRS frameworks.

The set of (to some degree) parallel processes – budget processes, PER/MTEF processes, sector strategies and strategic plans, and PRS processes – have developed over time with different starting points. The 2004 country study recommends (as we believed was planned) that it **might be useful to take the opportunity of the three-year PRS review to see if these various processes could be rationalised to some degree and integrated together better**. The PER evaluation carried out by the World Bank in 2004 makes some useful suggestions for streamlining and better integrating the annual PER/MTEF, PRS and budget processes, defining an annual cycle in which the PER/MTEF and PRSP progress report inform the December budget guidelines. **We suggest that the PRSP progress report should be produced each year in September/October, to feed into the MTEF, which should be produced around the same time – ahead of the budget guidelines issued in December.**

Capacity building for implementation

Experience to 2004 in Tanzania also emphasises the importance **of creating national capacity for undertaking the multiple functions required to implement a successful**

PRS. It is understandable that the initial focus was on building capacity for setting the strategy and engaging in debate with development partners and civil society. However, just as important is building capacity in sector ministries and at local level both to participate better in the strategy process and to implement it. At the same time **it is crucial**, as discussed in the next section, **to help free up government capacity by removing some of the demands – both of time and attention – placed on government by external partners.**

IV Quality of support given by development partners

How well are development partners supporting the PRS process?

Partners have given and continue to give much support to Tanzania's PRS process – for example, through their participation in the PRS Technical Committee, the PMS Steering Committee, the work of the PRS reviews and the various working groups of the PER/MTEF. At the same time, they provide support in building relevant government capacity: examples include the support from the World Bank and others for household budget surveys, which provide the key to better poverty monitoring; and support from the IMF, World Bank and others for a stronger public expenditure management capacity in the Ministry of Finance.

The Tanzania Assistance Strategy

The TAS and the TAS Implementation Action Plan are proving useful vehicles for driving the process of donor alignment and harmonisation, although ambition had been relatively modest to 2004. The joint government/development partner TAS secretariat had also added value in providing a continuing mechanism of consultations between government and the development partners. However, the frequency of its meetings in 2003 (two meetings instead of four, as envisaged) may have been a reflection of the need for further rationalisation of the consultation processes between government and development partners. **We see considerable scope for strengthening the TAS to incorporate some of the proposals made below for improving the modality and predictability of external support, and simplifying mechanisms for discussion and consultation with partners.** In general, aligning donor support better with country priorities set out in the PRS is likely to take time if it is to be sustainable, involving as it does reconciling systems and priorities of individual donors with those of the government.

Joint Staff Assessments

Joint Staff Assessments (JSAs) by the World Bank and IMF of the PRSP and annual progress reports, while perhaps less than fully candid, have helped improve the process. For example, the second progress report included for the first time an adequate macroeconomic analysis, linking macro policy with growth and poverty reduction, as recommended in the JSA on the initial PRSP. Another theme of development partners' comments on the content of PRS documents was the need for greater attention to accelerating growth and stepping up efforts towards domestic resource mobilisation – which was followed up in PRSP progress reports. **We believe these assessments can** continue to play a useful role both in informing decisions about international financial institution (IFI) financial commitments and providing feedback to the Government of Tanzania. However, to do so they should be candid, should focus on the whole PRS process, including implementation arrangements, and should draw on (or at least report) the views of other development partners. It follows from an earlier proposal that JSAs should no longer be linked to any appearance of BWI 'approval' of the PRS. They should be carried out to a timetable linked to government decisions and detached from BWI board schedules – perhaps produced on a regular annual basis at the time of the budget.

Have development partners accepted government priorities and policies as the basis for their support? Or have they sought additional conditions?

In general, partners seem increasingly ready to leave the Government of Tanzania the space it needs to produce its own strategy. Even the initial PRS, which sought to a large extent to follow a Washington 'template', marked a major advance from the days when country 'policy framework papers' were written in Washington. At the same time, by 2004 the government was clearly taking firm control of production of the PRS review. There is broad recognition that enhanced transparency and participation have strengthened national ownership and helped put the government in the driving seat.

Shift to budget support

One highly positive development has been the shift away from support for individual projects, each requiring separate negotiation and not always within the government's priorities, towards general budget support and support for sector strategies through basket funding arrangements. Donors who see the greatest difficulties in moving towards budget support or basket funding for sector strategies rather than individual projects are nonetheless beginning to do so. Peer pressure has helped encourage this development, as has observation of the qualitative benefits of programme and budget support, including its contribution to strengthening ownership.

Conditionality: imposed or government owned?

Despite the above, Tanzania is still a long way from a situation where development partners simply accept the government's priorities and support them. Donors supporting individual projects still insist on the normal array of project requirements, and not all projects fit with national priorities. As noted in section II, as of 2003, very little use was being made of the facility to fund projects through the budget. Basket-funding arrangements have been beset with delays resulting from difficulties in complying with requirements of some donors – though these are as often more to do with accounting and auditing procedures than being policy related. The IMF still negotiates the letter of intent written to gain access to the PRGF. Meanwhile, the group of donors providing budget support – the PRBS group – has set out its own conditions – summarised in a performance-assessment framework – in their collective discussions with government. Seen from the government's point of view, this collective discussion is preferable to a series of individual discussions with different donors, although it has imposed initial co-ordination burdens on government. It is also welcome that the PRBS group (which includes the World Bank, but not the IMF) has sought to align its conditions with those attached to the World Bank's PRSC and the IMF's PRGF. **However, while these various conditions and requirements set by development partners no doubt reflect genuine concerns, they seem less than fully consistent with the underlying spirit of the PRS approach.**

As noted elsewhere, there is bound to be some tension where a single strategy serves both as a national policy framework and as the basis for a contract with development partners. The question is, how is the tension being handled: how far do the 'conditions' attached to the PRSC and PRGF represent elaborations of the PRS made and accepted by the government; and how far, if at all, do they represent additions, outside the PRS, required by development partners as conditions for their support? The former would be within the broad spirit of the PRS approach, the latter would not, and some evidence suggests that the former is the more accurate model (see box 2.6).

Possible improvements

Our impression is that development partners' concerns in the provision of budget support are more to do with uncertainty about PRS implementation than questioning or seeking to add to the PRS itself. The key to reducing this kind of micro-management by donors may lie in a combination of greater self-restraint by donors (focusing only on issues they see as of major concern), reform of government implementation and decision and financial management processes, as discussed above, and better data about outturns and intermediate outputs. This would allow all to be assured that the PRS is being implemented effectively. The planned streamlining of government decision-making procedures should both reduce the number of occasions when inputs are needed and give greater clarity about the points in decision-making where constructive interventions by partners would be most useful. There is also a need to strengthen performance and results-oriented accountability arrangements, with a greater focus on outcomes as a way of reducing micro-management. The work that is being done under

---

Box 2.6: The June 2003 letter of intent

A comparison between the second PRSP progress report dated March 2003 and the macro-economic programme set out in the Government of Tanzania's letter of intent to the IMF dated 10 July 2003 throws some light on the question of the extent to which conditions are imposed rather than representing aspects of pre-existing government strategy.

The latter (see table 2 in the letter of intent) focuses on the areas of tax policy and tax administration, financial sector reform, the investment environment and governance. All these concerns are also reflected in varying degrees in the second PRSP progress report (pp. 17–26) – with tax issues, the investment environment (private-sector development) and governance given extensive discussion. These issues are also highlighted in the 'policy matrix for poverty reduction strategy, 2002/05' at the end of the second PRSP progress report document.

Hence there does seem to be a quite close correspondence between the PRGF 'conditions' and policies set out by the Government of Tanzania previously as its own priorities. Similarly, the PAF underlying support from the PRSC and PRBS group relates quite closely to items in the action matrix included in the second PRSP progress report.

Learning from Experience

the Public Service Reform Programme should be seen as an integral part of this reorientation.

Similar and if anything more acute issues arise in the operation of 'basket funds' at the sector level, with development partners still looking for auditing, monitoring and progress reporting arrangements separate from the government's own systems, despite reforms of the latter. Again the key to reducing donor micro-management may lie in further strengthening government processes and (perhaps as important) a better understanding by donors of what these processes are. The initiatives that Tanzania's Ministry of Finance has taken in this direction were already helping at the time of the study, but this would be an important area for attention in a strengthened TAS.

We also hope there can be rapid progress to a situation where those issues and actions that particular partners or groups of partners wish to highlight in more detail than in the PRS are handled by setting out the government's commitments in government policy statements and documents, rather than as separate negotiated 'conditions' for support. Some could and should feature in the PRSP itself. Others would feature in sector strategies or strategy plans. Others could be set out in self-standing government documents. For example, many of the actions and timetables in the PRBS PAF could, perhaps, be incorporated in the PRSP itself; and future letters of intent to the IMF might be written not as extended letters from the minister, but as a short covering letter attaching a published document setting out the government's priorities and policy commitments in macroeconomic policy. **Making commitments in this way in public and to parliament, rather than in semi-private negotiated documents, would be an important part of strengthening domestic accountability.**

Is financial support becoming more predictable? Are donor decisions and disbursements timed to coincide with the budget cycle?

The move to budget support financing has been associated with a significant improvement in the short-term predictability of disbursements, as reflected in their timing. In contrast to the past, when most disbursements were in the final quarter of the FY, approaching 60 per cent of budget support was by 2004 disbursed in the first quarter, with 90 per cent scheduled for disbursement by the end of the second quarter. Greater familiarisation with and reliance on the government's own financial control mechanisms have been a major contributing factor. This is true of much multilateral as well as bilateral support. At the time of writing, the move to basket funding at the sector level had yet to pay similar dividends in terms of timing and front loading of disbursements, although the outcome tends to be better where sector-development plans are better programmed and agreed upon with development partners. Sector ministries often express a preference for basket funding, which they see as a basis for a close relationship with development partners, giving them some independence from central government budget decisions. On the other hand, they also express a preference in terms of usability and predictability for finance provided through the budget over both basket funding and project finance.

However, despite its many advantages, there are real concerns about the medium-term predictability and reliability of budget support finance, where there is a perceived risk of delay or non-disbursement by donors because of relatively modest policy disagreements or political events including events outside the government's control. In the words of the June 2003 Action Plan for implementing the TAS, 'The risks of non-disbursement or untimely disbursement are particularly acute for direct budget support, where government may have committed funds in good faith, based on agreed expectations of disbursements. Increased transparency and timely sharing of information will reduce problems associated with predictability.'

Our view is that those providing budget support should be prepared to go further. In effect they are committing themselves to give general financial support for implementing the PRS – and as that is a medium-term strategy, their commitment should be medium term also, perhaps set out in the form of a rolling multi-year 'contract' setting out support to be expected, with disbursements only disrupted in the most serious circumstances, including serious failure to implement the PRS.

How well is donor co-ordination and harmonisation working?

By the time of writing, development partners in Tanzania had made considerable progress in implementing the 'Rome' agenda of better donor co-ordination and harmonisation, but there was still much more to be done.

Donor missions

The impressive array of local co-ordinating and consultation committees and groups has not yet eliminated the need for individual donor missions, contacts and negotiations with the GoT – though it should be a long-term objective that it should do so. Indeed, in FY2002/03 the government estimated there were more than 500 separate missions from partners, many from donors like the World Bank with a substantial local presence. As of 2004, some progress had been made in declaring quiet periods of the year, when missions are not welcome. Where such missions are purely technical they can of course add value, bringing in expertise. The problem arises when – as is too often the case – visiting officials feel they need to take up the time of senior officials and ministers.

Local consultation machinery

On the other hand, the multiplicity of local co-ordinating mechanisms, both for the overall strategy and at the sectoral and cross-cutting issues level, is also a matter of concern – both to donors and even more so to the government, given time and capacity constraints in government departments. Although this was perhaps a necessary response to the inherent tensions in the PRS process and to the initial challenges of implementing the 'Rome' agenda, **some rationalisation was already overdue by 2004.** Development partners had begun a rationalisation process, asking each of the development partner groups and working parties listed in their December 2003 stocktake to justify their continued existence. A more radical approach may be needed, perhaps with the GoT in the lead. This might be linked to the strengthening of PRS implementation and budget processes in government discussed above. At the national level, the Development Co-operation Forum appeared to be defunct by the time of the study, and questions were also being asked about the value added from consultative group meetings, formally the apex of the donor co-ordination effort. In view of the strengthening of the TAS and the new institutional arrangements that have been created to implement it, it may also be necessary to revisit the role of the consultative group.

Local presence of development partners

A related issue is whether all partners are correctly organised at local level to allow the kind of effective local dialogue implicit in the PRS process, and to permit the phasing out of separate inward missions. **Our own view is that given the scale of external support for Tanzania and the spirit of the PRS approach and the Rome harmonisation and alignment agenda, all significant development partners, including the IMF, need to organise themselves locally so they can engage effectively in policy discussion in-country, and that this should lead to a significant reduction in the number and frequency of visiting missions.** In some cases this may require more local staff, but more importantly **it will require empowerment of local staff by head offices to take decisions locally; better arrangements for continuity when local staff rotate; and implementation of arrangements for specialisation among development partners, assigning different partners the acknowledged lead in different sectors or issues.** Taken together with the rationalisation of local consultation mechanisms suggested here, this would result in a significantly reduced burden on government.

Would higher levels of assistance be useful?

The case for larger donor flows needs to be addressed in the context of a broadened PRS making it more of a comprehensive development programme, Tanzania's absorptive capacity, and concerns about 'Dutch disease' – when too large a flow of external assistance leads to too high an exchange rate. The government and some donors stress the need for an exit strategy from aid dependence, and this is clearly a correct long-term goal. **However, in the short to medium term, there are a number of factors that suggest that in Tanzania a steady increase in volumes of aid would be productive and effective in driving progress to meeting the Millennium Development Goals (MDGs) in the country.** First, levels of aid in relation to GDP are not particularly high by historic standards. Second, there has been no sign so far of aid inflows affecting the exchange rate, and in general higher flows seem likely to be matched by higher imports. Third, as the PRS is broadened to cover new sectors, and effective strategies evolve for those sectors, there will be more areas where financial support would be helpful. Fourth, there is already a well-developed set of mechanisms for handling aid flows – particularly those that pass through the budget – and the associated policy dialogue with development partners, which form a good basis for handling extra flows of aid. Absorptive capacities would of course need to be further addressed, with challenges in terms of capacity building and utilisation of allocated resources, which suggests it would be more realistic to think in terms of a steady build up in volume rather than a step change.

A strengthened Tanzania Assistance Strategy

We suggest that all these proposals should be underpinned (as we believe was planned at the time of writing) by a revised and strengthened Tanzania Assistance Strategy (TAS). Work by development partners to develop a new 'joint assistance strategy' (JAS) provides a good opportunity to make progress, and draw up a new TAS. This would need to address:

- Issues related to basket and project funding to the public sector – unless these can be phased out in favour of budget support
- Reducing the points and occasions for policy engagement
- Increasing the predictability of budget support, as proposed earlier

The need for independent monitoring

A unique feature of the development process in Tanzania is the arrangement for carrying out a periodic independent assessment of how the process is working, through the Independent Monitoring Group (IMG). It is widely accepted that the reports from this group continue to add value. It is an arrangement that might usefully be replicated in other countries. It is important, however, that the IMG's recommendations should either be acted upon or that clear reasons should be given where action is not taken.

V Main findings and recommendations

Successes and areas for attention in the PRS process in Tanzania

To summarise, experience with developing and implementing the Tanzanian Poverty Reduction Strategy has been generally positive. It benefited from a number of pre-existing and parallel processes in the United Republic of Tanzania, and evolved during the first three years of implementation in ways that improved the process and pointed to further changes needed in future, many of them already under way. As the government completed its review and prepared its new PRS, we saw scope for improvements in five areas, recognising that in many cases steps were already being taken to introduce such changes along the lines suggested.

Establishing full national ownership

There is a need to further broaden ownership, strengthen domestic accountability and embed the PRS and its implementation better in national processes, including the budget process. It is important to remove the perception of the PRS being primarily linked to the provision of external support and to establish the PRS as the central national framework for growth and poverty reduction.

We would like to emphasise in particular the importance of **action to increase awareness of the PRS among parliamentarians and local councillors and their involvement in the process.** True national 'ownership' of the process would and should be reflected in increased accountability to the people, and greater involvement of parliament, as was beginning to happen in the PRS review, seems crucial to the political sustainability of the process. Similarly, it is important to achieve greater awareness of the process and involvement among local councillors, who are responsible for the local development machinery. Other parallel actions may be needed to help establish the PRS as the guiding national strategy, including, for example, **more frequent high-level policy statements giving it this status and adopting a new national name for the strategy.**

At the same time, a **particular area where the quality of participation and discussion needs to be improved is in relation to macroeconomic policy.** The technical nature of some macro-policy issues should not be seen as a reason for limiting debate.

The PRS should be both a national strategy and also accepted by development partners as the basis for their support. **In due course there should be little or no need for separate conditionalities negotiated with partners.** All government commitments/agreed actions should be set out either in the PRS itself or in parallel more detailed public government policy statements. **Nor should the PRS as a national, government approved policy document, be subjected to a process that gives the appearance of requiring external approvals by the IMF and World Bank, or any other external partners.** Obviously BWIs and other external partners have to make their own decisions about how much support to give, but it is important to avoid any appearance of giving BWI 'approval'. This may require changes in BWI procedures, which in any event should focus more on assessing the whole PRS process, including implementation arrangements, and much less on the quality of individual documents.

Joint Staff Assessments carried out by the BWIs of the PRSP and PRSP progress reports would then cease to be linked to any concept of BWI 'approval'. JSAs would still be useful, both in informing decisions in the BWIs about the degree and nature of their support, and in providing feedback to the country. However, to fulfil these functions effectively, JSAs need to be candid, focus on the whole PRS process (including implementation), draw on or report the views of other development partners, and be carried out to a timetable linked to government decisions rather than BWI board schedules – perhaps produced on a regular annual basis at the time of the budget.

Establishing the PRS as a comprehensive strategy for growth and poverty reduction

It was hoped that the new PRS would complete the process already begun, of transforming what was originally a more narrowly focused strategy into a comprehensive national strategy for growth, development and poverty reduction.

We would like to emphasise in particular that:
- **A more comprehensive strategy does not mean sacrificing priority setting – indeed it makes it even more important to be explicit and specific about priorities.** However, priorities need to be set recognising the contribution of all sectors and policies to desired outcomes, and their interrelationships. This will also help to spread ownership of the PRS throughout government.
- **It should be made clear that the new PRS encompasses the recently published medium-term plan for growth and poverty reduction.**

Taken together with the actions set out above, these actions will all help the process of developing the PRS into what it should become: the central national framework for actions to support growth and poverty reduction.

Better integrating and simplifying national policy-making and implementation

Implementation of the PRS needs to be more fully integrated with national policy-making and budget processes, which themselves need to be streamlined and rationalised. This aspect was recognised in the Ministry of Finance, which had been working to rationalise all the related processes within the national budget and PRS frameworks.

A fully successful PRS process requires all related government processes to be linked together well, and all those concerned with its implementation to see the strategy as an integral part of the work of their ministries and institutions, not as a separate activity for which responsibility lies in the VPO or MoF. In particular:

- A firmer link between the PRS, sector strategies and budget decisions is needed. **We believe the 2004 PRS review could provide an opportunity to see if these various existing parallel processes could be rationalised and integrated together better.**
- **It is also important to build capacity across government, using increased support from development partners, to strengthen the government's ability to lead the process.** As important as building capacity are the steps discussed below for reducing some of the current demands of time and attention placed on government by development partners.

Aligning support from development partners with the PRS

While there had already been some progress at the time of country study, there is scope in Tanzania for much more to be done to align external support better with the country priorities set out in the PRS. This is a process likely to take some time if it is to be sustainable, involving as it does reconciling systems and priorities of donors with those of the government.

To make progress, **a combination of greater self-restraint by donors – focusing only on issues they see as of major concern – reform of government implementation and decision and financial management processes as discussed above, and better data about outturns and intermediate outputs** seems particularly important. This would allow all to be assured that the PRS is being implemented effectively. The planned streamlining of government decision-making procedures should both reduce the number of occasions when inputs are needed and give greater clarity about the points in decision-making where constructive interventions by partners would be most useful.

We also hoped that there could be rapid progress, as suggested above, to a situation where those issues and actions that particular partners or groups of partners wish to highlight in more detail than in the PRS are handled by setting them out as government commitments in government documents, rather than as separate negotiated 'conditions' for the IMF, World Bank and other external supporters.

In the short to medium term there are a number of factors that suggest that in Tanzania a steady increase in volumes of aid would be productive and effective in driving progress to meeting the MDGs.

Improving the modalities of external support

There was also a need to build further on past achievements in improving the modalities and effectiveness of external support, implementing in Tanzania the global 'Rome' agenda on aid harmonisation. We would like to highlight the following:

- The move to general budget support financing has many advantages. However, there were still substantial levels of funding to sector baskets and to individual projects at the time of writing. If these forms of financing continue, it is

Learning from Experience

important to ensure that they fall within overall government priorities and as far as possible are accounted for within government systems.

- There is a concern that despite its other advantages, budget financing could prove less stable and predictable than project finance. In particular, many see a risk that budget support donors could suspend their disbursements because of relatively modest policy disagreements or political events. **Those providing budget support are committing themselves to give general financial support for implementing the PRS – and as that is a medium-term strategy, their commitment should be medium term also, perhaps set out in the form of a rolling multi-year 'contract' setting out support to be expected, with disbursements only disrupted in the most serious circumstances.**

- The combination of continuing high levels of inward development partner missions and a highly elaborate system of local consultation machinery places high demands both on government and development partners. The best approach is to try to **focus more on local consultation, and at the same time take steps to rationalise local consultation machinery.**

- A closer development partnership on the ground in Tanzania requires changes from development partners. **All significant partners need to organise themselves locally so they can engage effectively in policy discussion in-country.** In some cases this may require more local staff, but more **importantly it requires empowerment of local staff by head offices to take decisions locally; better arrangements for continuity when local staff rotate; and implementation of arrangements for specialisation among development partners, assigning different partners the acknowledged lead in different sectors or issues.**

- We suggest underpinning these proposals – as we believe was already planned – with **a new and strengthened Tanzania Assistance Strategy.**

- This is also to be assisted by **continuing the arrangement for carrying out a periodic independent assessment of how the process is working, through the Independent Monitoring Group.** It is widely accepted that reports from this group continue to add value.

Lessons for other countries and for the international community

Many of these lessons from the Tanzanian experience may have relevance in other PRSP countries and for the international system. In this respect, we highlight the following:

- The whole PRS process, including implementation, is more important than individual documents. To be effective, PRSs need to be comprehensive, setting strategy for all policies relevant to growth and poverty reduction. They should also be fully integrated into the government systems for taking decisions, setting budgets and implementing policy, with ownership throughout government, not just in the central departments.

- Stronger engagement of parliaments is crucial if the process is to be politically sustainable.

- As PRSs develop, as they should, into central national development strategies covering all aspects of policy relevant to growth and poverty reduction, it appears increasingly inappropriate for there to be even the appearance of approval by BWIs.

- As PRSs develop into strategies accepted by development partners as a basis for their support, it should also be possible to move away from separate donor and agency negotiated conditionalities, with policies and commitments where necessary spelt out in greater detail than in the PRS in separate government policy documents.
- Some of the Tanzanian arrangements for monitoring and improving donor alignment and harmonisation, such as the TAS and IMG, might usefully be replicated in other countries.
- The trend to stronger local policy dialogue has important implications for development partners – notably the need for an empowered local presence to participate effectively, phasing out missions from capitals and head offices, and implementing local arrangements for different partners to take the lead on different issues.

Budget support finance has many advantages. To allay concerns about its medium-term predictability it should carry with it a medium-term commitment from development partners, with disbursements only to be disrupted in the most serious circumstances.

CHAPTER 3

Monitoring Donor and IFI Support Behind Country-owned Poverty Reduction Strategies in Ghana

Ernest Aryeetey and David Peretz

I   Introduction

This chapter presents the second of the country reports prepared under the Commonwealth Secretariat project to monitor implementation of the Poverty Reduction Strategy (PRS) process in Commonwealth countries. The report on Ghana was prepared by Professor Ernest Aryeetey, Director of the Institute of Statistical, Social and Economic Research (ISSER), University of Ghana, and David Peretz, a senior consultant and adviser to the Commonwealth Secretariat. This case study was completed in June 2005.

In preparing the report, we drew on a number of previous studies. We held a series of discussions in Ghana with representatives of government, the private sector, civil society and development partners, including a workshop and a second series of discussions to discuss a draft of the report. We also had discussions with officials of the IMF and World Bank. The conclusions are, however, our own. We focus this report and its findings on a set of key issues and questions developed as a template for the series of country reports. With at the time of the Ghana study only three years' experience of implementation of the Ghana Poverty Reduction Strategy (GPRS), it was too early to say much about final outcomes and results. The focus of this report, therefore, is more on processes and intermediate outcomes.

The chapter is organised as follows. Section II describes the PRS process as it evolved and continues to evolve in Ghana. Section III examines issues to do with the strategy itself and its implementation. Section IV discusses the quality of support being given by development partners. Section V summarises key findings and recommendations.

II   Evolution of the Ghana Poverty Reduction Strategy

Origins of the GPRS

The first Ghana Poverty Reduction Strategy (GPRS) was prepared by the Government of Ghana in consultation with the World Bank, the IMF and other development partners as part of the global initiative to introduce poverty reduction strategies within the development assistance framework. After three years of implementing the first programme under the strategy, an update of the GPRS was under preparation, and a first consultation draft was scheduled to be ready at the end of June 2005.

The first GPRS ('An Agenda for Growth and Prosperity') is a comprehensive policy document intended to guide and support growth and poverty reduction activities over the period to 2005. The document provides policies, programmes and projects judged by the various stakeholders to be essential in improving the development of the country on a sustainable basis through 'wealth creation for the benefit of all Ghanaians'. The document outlines strategies and targets to achieve growth and reduce poverty, first providing an overview of the macroeconomic situation, structural and social policies in support of growth and poverty reduction, as well as associated domestic and external financing needs, while identifying the major sources of finance. The GPRS is also intended to ensure that all Ghanaians have access to basic social services such as health care, quality education, potable drinking water, decent housing, security from crime and violence, as well as the ability to participate in decision-making.

It is important to underscore the fact that the adoption of the GPRS in 2003, reflects a series of activities associated with Ghana's long-term development ideals, relationships with donors or development partners and changes in global governance arrangements. In this section we discuss events leading to the preparation of the GPRS, the processes used for its preparation and an overview of its contents.

Long-term development strategies before the GPRS

One of the biggest problems that the economy of Ghana has faced in the last two decades has been the difficulty in dealing with adverse terms of trade shocks, which would suggest a major failure after almost two decades of macroeconomic reform. To tackle the problem, towards the end of the 1980s, the authorities began to consider various options for structural transformation that would make the economy more robust. A National Development Planning Commission (NDPC) was set up and charged with the responsibility of preparing a long-term development framework, to be implemented in a number of medium-term phases. This resulted in the development of a 'Ghana: Vision 2020' document, with a first medium-term plan that covered the period 1996–2000. This was done fully cognisant of the failures of the 1960s' attempts at long-term planning, which focused on significant public-sector participation and a determination not to repeat those mistakes. There was a desire to emulate what were perceived to be the indicative roles of the state in bringing about structural transformation in East Asia.

Various reports from both the Ghana government and independent sources have suggested that the implementation of Ghana: Vision 2020 was haphazard at best. The planning commission was poorly equipped to carry out the tasks assigned to it, and the decentralised public-administration system continued to function under a lot of strain as a result of both financial and other institutional inadequacies (NDPC, 2001). An important weakness related to the lack of clarity on the role of the district assemblies, as central government institutions continued to be the agencies for the most significant public expenditures on social and economic infrastructure, a fact which continued to affect the efficiency of such expenditures (NDPC, 2001). Despite rapidly rising capital expenditures in the 1990s, their impact on rural development and poverty reduction remained questionable (Wetzel, 2000). Moreover, progress was also set back by imprudent budget expansions prior to elections in 1996 and 2000.

In early 2000, the government began the process of putting in place a second medium-term programme (MTP) under Ghana: Vision 2020. After this process was launched, the government also agreed with its development partners to prepare a Poverty Reduction Strategy Paper in the new international spirit of putting in place PRSPs for developing countries. The domestic debate at the time among government officials and donors was whether to let the MTP inform the PRSP or vice versa. The view tended to be that the MTP reflected a broader development strategy, which should guide the PRSP. The two processes ran in parallel, with occasional consultations in order to inform both processes. Thus the Interim PRSP (I-PRSP) emphasised economic growth with integrated rural development; the expansion of employment opportunities; and improved access to basic public services such as education, health care, water and sanitation and family planning services. However, neither of these processes were completed before a change in government with the elections of December 2000.

The I-PRSP was perceived to have had very little local ownership in view of the major roles donors played in getting it started and supporting it. The document was also seen to have unrealistic implementation strategies and inadequate financing. Nonetheless, the authorities' attitude to a PRSP soon changed.

Factors leading to the adoption of the Ghana Poverty Reduction Strategy

Shortly after the 2000 elections, officials of the new government indicated, unofficially, that Ghana: Vision 2020 had been abandoned. While the government itself did not state categorically any position on the status of the Vision, this disregard for it soon became apparent. It is thought the new government perceived the processes relating to the Vision to have been politicised. What the abandonment of the Vision implied was that the preparations for a full poverty reduction strategy were also suspended.

The pressure for instituting a new PRSP came from donors, who conditioned debt relief through a HIPC programme on the pursuit of poverty-reducing activities on the basis of a PRSP. It may be noted that for several weeks after the new regime came into office, the government indicated that it was studying critically the issue of whether Ghana should opt for HIPC debt relief or not. This debate took place publicly for several weeks, with indications of clear division among government ministers and other politicians, and even among the public. Interestingly, the debate immediately ended with the visit of the UK Secretary of State for International Development in early 2001, which was largely perceived by the public to have given the government a strong signal that there would be no major assistance from development partners without a HIPC agreement. Since the HIPC agreement was predicated on a strong and acceptable PRSP, the National Development Planning Commission was once again given the instruction to prepare a PRSP. Thus, it was the need for immediate debt relief that eventually forced a new interest in developing a PRSP, but this time without the broader development framework of Ghana: Vision 2020 as its anchor.

Under the current strategy, the government has maintained that it is more focused on creating wealth by transforming the economy to achieve growth. This is more in line with the party's political ideology of having private sector-led growth in a market-based economy, although accelerated poverty reduction and the protection of the vulnerable and excluded within a decentralised and democratic environment are also given emphasis. In the discussions for a second GPRS, the attention to growth has been strengthened even further and the 'G' in the acronym is being translated to mean 'growth'.

III Preparation and content of the GPRS

Both in the process for drawing up the GPRS and in its content, officials of the National Development Planning Commission sought to take into account the various weaknesses of earlier strategy documents. The document itself provides extensive discussion of poverty, and sets out strategies intended to ensure that macroeconomic stability and the framework for economic growth support poverty reduction.

For the preparation of the document, five core teams were established to manage the five thematic areas of the GPRS, namely: macroeconomy; production and gainful employment; human resource development and basic services; vulnerability and exclusion; and governance. The teams comprised representatives of appropriate government ministries, civil society organisations, non-governmental organisations, the private sector, development partners and some private individuals.

The NDPC maintains that the GPRS was formulated through a fairly transparent and participatory process as demanded by the guidelines of the international financial institutions (IFIs). This was to ensure ownership, transparency and accountability of the policy document. The process of the sequential preparation of the document by the NDPC was officially outlined as follows:

- Five core teams were established for macroeconomic issues, production and gainful employment, human resource development and basic services, vulnerability and exclusion and governance. This initial stage was based on the preliminary findings of a task force of consultants.
- Local-level consultations were held on dimensions of poverty and recommended solutions involving a sample of 36 communities in 12 districts and six administrative regions.
- Consultations were held among core teams and key agencies on analysis of data from local consultations and quantitative data-gathering exercises, leading to identification of priority issues and required actions for poverty reduction.
- A forum of civil society, private sector bodies, government agencies and development partners was held to review and harmonise priority issues and actions.
- A special forum for civil society was organised to validate priority issues and actions.
- A review and prioritisation was organised at the national economic dialogue, comprising representatives of development stakeholders in Ghana.

At the national economic dialogue, the conclusion was drawn that the GPRS document addressed the challenges facing the country with respect to poverty reduction and growth. The first draft of the document was made public in mid-May 2001, after key government agencies had looked over it and given their technical inputs. Other development stakeholders, including planning and budget staff of ministries, departments and agencies were also consulted for their contributions during a week-long training workshop on the process and content of the poverty-reduction policy framework. This was followed by discussions with development partners forming five working groups to comment on the first draft document in July 2001. Consultation workshops were held with several different groups including the Trades' Union Congress and Civil Society

Coalition, women's groups, the media, Ghana Association of Private Voluntary Organisations in Development, policy activists and independent think tanks. Other groups were the Ghana Employers' Association, the Private Enterprise Foundation, the Association of Ghana Industries, the Ghana National Chamber of Mines, the National Union of Ghana Students, the National Association of Local Governments, public ministries, departments and agencies and identified individuals in the development arena. After all of these consultations, the cabinet also reviewed the document.

The Finance and Public Accounts Committees of the Parliament of Ghana each held one-day workshops to deliberate on the draft GPRS. The final document was then laid before the entire parliament for approval. A forum for all political parties was also held to seek the views and comments of the various political groups on the GPRS. The president held a two-day meeting with all the ministers to discuss the content and scope of the draft strategy, as well as the expenditure shares for the administrative categories. Another meeting by the president and his ministers was held in January 2002 for review and costing of the GPRS, which was completed in February 2002 for inclusion in the 2002 budget statement. However, this initial 2002 GPRS was not properly prioritised and partners, not least the IMF, had a strong say in the production of a revised, prioritised version eventually adopted by the government, presented to parliament and endorsed by the boards of the IMF and the World Bank in 2003. There have been several discussions of the issue of ownership in relation to the stage at which the Bretton Woods institutions came into the picture and the extent of their involvement. There was often the argument among Ghanaians interviewed that the influence of the IFIs in prioritising the strategy was considerable, and did not necessarily reflect the national development priorities. The argument made by Jeffrey Sachs (2003) in Accra in this regard has been that the development partners only sought to achieve an outcome that was compatible with their resource envelope, without giving Ghana the option of seeking or developing additional resources for the task of sustainable development.

Turning to the content, the GPRS sets out a strategy for poverty reduction including: ensuring macroeconomic stability through prudent fiscal, monetary and international trade policies; increasing production and gainful employment through an enabling environment for improved private sector-led agro-based industrial production driven by the application of science and technology and the promotion of tourism; human development and provision of basic services through increased and improved access to and utilisation of basic services by the poor, especially in regards to health, HIV/AIDS control, population management, water and sanitation, education and training; special programmes for the vulnerable and excluded through the provision of resources and measures to promote gender balance and equity, expansion of the social security scheme coverage and introduction of mutual health insurance to cover a majority of workers; and good governance through the establishment and strengthening of the leadership and oversight functions of the executive and parliament.

Integration of the GPRS into the national policy-making framework

Fully integrating the GPRS into the national policy-making framework has proved a difficult and ongoing process. One set of difficulties is constitutional. The government sees the GPRS as the central medium-term strategy for development, supplemented by a range of sectoral and cross-sectoral strategies. The Co-ordinated Programme for

Economic and Social Development (CPESD), which is constitutionally mandated, might appear to be a rival process, although in practice it appears to have little operational significance (and it includes some actions to address poverty, such as housing, which are not, but probably should be, included in the GPRS). Moreover, the constitution makes clear what processes are to be used in generating development priorities, including the establishment of a decentralised planning framework, which matches a decentralised governance structure that promotes strong local government through partially elected district assemblies. It envisages that there will be district development plans, based on which national medium-term development priorities will be developed to form the basis of a medium-term expenditure framework (MTEF). In practice, the GPRS was initiated outside of the arrangements anticipated under the constitution and other development planning laws. As a result, the methods for linking it with other public planning were ad hoc, and often not clearly understood by implementing agencies.

Thus in practice the Government of Ghana developed an MTEF and its three-year medium-term priorities (MTPs) for the period 2002–2004 without any significant reference to the district assemblies. The process had to be fast-tracked in order to match the timing of the GPRS after it had already begun. The MTPs include consideration of

---

Box 3.1 Objectives of Ghana's medium-term priorities (MTPs)

- To open up the country, introduce competition and create an enabling environment for the private sector through the improvement of infrastructure. Activities that would facilitate the achievement of this objective included: the construction of major highways as well as link up with the trans-ECOWAS highway project and a major road to a productive area in every region in the country; acceleration of further development of ports through private-sector participation; improvement of telecommunication accessibility; and the increase of the availability of energy to boost industrial growth and production.
- To develop the country so that it would become an agro-industrial economy by the year 2010 through modernised agriculture based on rural development. The government hoped to achieve this objective through: land acquisition reforms for easy access and efficient land ownership and title process; assisting the private sector to increase the production of grains and tubers for food security, as well as cash crops through research services, irrigation and affordable credit facilities; and supporting the private sector to add value to traditional crops such as cocoa.
- To enhance the delivery of social services to ensure locational equity and quality, mainly with regards to education and health. This would seek to: change the educational system to facilitate uninterrupted education for all Ghanaians from pre-school to age 17; develop a model health centre and senior secondary school in every district in the country; and phase out the 'cash-and-carry' system for health charges payment.
- To ensure the rule of law, respect for human rights and the attainment of social justice and equity by strengthening the three arms of government – the executive, the judiciary and the legislature. This would be done through: support for the work of parliament; restructuring the civil service to ensure efficiency and effectiveness; strengthening the capacity of the Attorney-General and the judiciary; enhancing social order by improving the police service by equipping them with vehicles, communications equipment and technology, enhancing their training and increasing their numbers; and ensuring transparency and accountability in resource generation, allocation and management.
- To strengthen the private sector in an active way to ensure that it is capable of acting effectively as the engine of growth and poverty reduction.

Learning from Experience

infrastructure, modernised agriculture based on rural development, enhanced social services, good governance and private-sector development. The objectives of the MTPs appear to be to a degree aligned with those in the GPRS, but the match is by no means perfect.

The guidelines for the MTPs were prepared through consultation between the NDPC, responsible for the GPRS, the Budget Division of the Ministry of Finance and the medium-term expenditure framework secretariat. Implementation of the GPRS was intended to assist in achieving the medium-term priorities, and a large part of the GPRS was to be funded under the MTEF, assuming convergence between the GPRS and the MTPs.

In practice, while a degree of convergence may exist, this has proved difficult. A number of the ministries, departments and agencies (MDAs), including health and education, concede that it has not been easy to align their programmes under the MTEF with the framework of GPRS – a process made even more difficult with operational problems of the MTEF. There are also disconnects in the further process of linking the MTEF with annual budgets. In short, linking the GPRS to the budgetary process has been problematic, although MDAs suggested that they were beginning to get a handle on the problems by the time the Ghana study was undertaken.

Progress in implementing the GPRS: annual progress reports

The implementation of the GPRS started in 2002 (before final adoption of the strategy in 2003) with the understanding that it would be updated regularly by relying on the contents of a comprehensive monitoring and evaluation system and leading to an annual progress report (APR). The monitoring and evaluation exercise was expected to inform Ghanaians about whether targets were achieved or not, so that corrective action could be taken well before the end of the GPRS period, if necessary. The APR provides a framework for the systematic review of the GPRS programme and project implementation, as well as their impact on socio-economic development for the year. It also provides feedback for future policy-making and implementation. The APR uses the MTPs, and the relevant 52 indicators identified in the GPRS monitoring and evaluation plan, as its main frame of reference. The APR also comments on the status of the GPRS-based triggers and targets for assessing performance in the donor support programmes, such as the Poverty Reduction Support Credit (PRSC); the Multi-Donor Budget Support programme (MDBS) and the Poverty Reduction and Growth Facility (PRGF) as well as for meeting the floating targets for the HIPC completion point. The APR assesses performance in achieving the Millennium Development Goals. It uses earlier surveys by the Ghana Statistical Service (GSS), as well as two new surveys conducted by the GSS in the first quarter of 2003, the Core Welfare Indicator Questionnaire (CWIQ) and the Ghana Demographic and Health Survey. At the time of the country report highlighted here, Ghana had had two APRs, for 2002 and 2003.

The first APR in 2002 focused on the implementation of the medium-term priority programmes, mainly consisting of sector programmes and projects and concentrated on the establishment of baseline data to form the basis for future monitoring and evaluation. The 2003 report provided a more comprehensive assessment of progress. As pointed out by the Institute of Statistical Social and Economic Research (ISSER, 2005), the major challenge of the APRs is the lack of consistent and reliable data and the lack of harmonisation in data from the various sector ministries, departments and agencies that provide inputs for the APR. Other challenges include: problems related to accuracy and timeliness of data from primary and secondary sources; lack of motivation for staff in the MDAs and districts to institutionalise the collection and provision of data; infrequent national outcome/impact surveys by the GSS due to inadequate resources; and the challenge of reporting on multiple indicator/trigger achievements for a number of programmes, such as the GPRS, MTPs, PRSC, MDBS, HIPC and MDGs.

In fact evidence of the impact of the GPRS on the composition of the budget has been reasonably strong in some respects, but less so in others. According to government budget figures, the budget allocation for administration declined from 19.79 per cent in 2002 to 14.84 per cent in 2003, which was close to the GPRS target of 14.2 per cent. The social-service sector allocation increased consistently to 38.67 per cent from the beginning of the implementation of the GPRS, which was slightly higher than the GPRS target of 38.1 per cent. The social-service resources increase translated into an increase in the allocation to the vulnerable and excluded, education and health, emphasising the importance of social-service access and delivery as the core of the GPRS. Expenditure on infrastructure increased from 11.64 per cent in 2001 to 17.2 per cent in 2002, and declined to 15.5 per cent in 2003, which was lower than the projected GPRS target of 17.2 per cent. The allocation for the public-safety sector, however, increased from 9.67 per cent in 2002 to 11.52 per cent in 2003, exceeding the GPRS target of 11.1 per cent. The government saw the increased allocation to the public-safety sector as reflecting the importance of upholding the rule of law, public order and safety as major pillars of the GPRS. On the other hand, the allocation to economic services declined by almost 50 per cent, falling from 18.02 per cent in 2002 to 9.06 per cent in 2003: as this includes expenditure on agriculture (about half), this drop may have had significant negative implications for the poverty-reduction programme.

Experience with GPRS outcomes

By the time the Ghana study was conducted in 2005, it was still much too early to make a proper assessment of the success or failure of the GPRS in terms of final results. This country report therefore focus mainly on issues of process and intermediate outcomes.

Box 3.2 Institutional arrangements for monitoring and evaluation

The National Development Planning Commission (NDPC) is the main institution responsible for the monitoring and evaluation of the GPRS. It is supported by the National Intra-Agency Poverty Monitoring Groups (NIPMG), the GPRS Strategic Environment Assessment Group, the GPRS Dissemination Committee and the Poverty and Social Impact Assessment, Technical and Advisory Committees.

The NIPMG involves five groups based on the GPRS thematic areas. The groups are inter-sectoral and involve both governmental and non-governmental representatives selected for their knowledge of the respective thematic area. The members are from the policy, planning, monitoring and evaluation divisions of the various MDAs, Development Agency staff, the GSS and selected researchers. Their functions include highlighting the importance of monitoring and evaluation of the GPRS within the relevant MDAs; providing data towards an update of the selected indicators and policy interventions; and reviewing and validating data, as well as policy recommendations.

Nonetheless, the following paragraphs seek to identify some of the achievements identified in the report.

In the short- to medium-term (2003–2005) real GDP growth was expected to rise from 4.7 per cent in 2003 to about 5 per cent in 2005; agricultural growth from 4.1 per cent per annum in 2002 to 4.8 per cent per annum by 2005; and the service sector was expected to have a growth rate of 5.1 per cent in 2005 relative to the 4.7 per cent growth rate in 2002. An inflation target was set at 5.0 per cent in 2005, with credit to government targeted to decline from a growth rate of 32.5 per cent in 2002 to 0 per cent in 2003 and –7.7 per cent in 2005. All the above targets were set with an underlying assumption that there would be no sustained domestic and/or external shocks.

At the time of writing, the macroeconomic indicators showed macro stability to be on track. The 5.2 per cent growth rate of GDP in 2003 exceeded the target of 4.7 per cent set at the beginning of the year and the 4.9 per cent target of the GPRS. In 2004, GDP growth was 5.8 per cent, which was 0.6 percentage points higher than the expected growth. The domestic debt/GDP ratio decreased from 29.1 per cent in 2002 to 22.6 per cent in 2003 and partly contributed to a reduction in inflation and a decline in interest rates. Growth of credit to the private sector also increased from –11 per cent in 2001 to 37.5 per cent in 2003. The budget deficit declined from 6.8 per cent in 2002 to 4.9 per cent of GDP in 2003, against a target of 4.3 per cent. The inflation rate was at 23.6 per cent at the end of 2003, against a target of 9.0 per cent, due to a 90.4 per cent increase in petroleum prices at the beginning of 2003. This went up again in 2004 (see table 3.1 for a summary of Ghana's macroeconomic situation.)

The annual progress reports provide some information on the development outcomes. The proposed outcomes from the GPRS can be looked at from the point of view

Table 3.1: Macroeconomic trends under GPRS I

Indicator	2002	2003		2004	
(% unless otherwise stated)	Actual	Target	Actual	Target	Actual
National GDP					
Nominal GDP (¢ billion)	47,764	65,262	66,158	77,620	79,803
Real GDP growth	4.5	4.7	5.2	5.2	5.8
Real per capita GDP growth	1.9		2.5		3.1
Sectoral growth rates					
Agriculture	4.4	4.5	6.1	6.0	7.5
Industry	4.7	5.1	5.1	5.2	5.1
Services	4.7	4.9	4.7	4.7	4.7
Fiscal indicators					
Domestic revenue/GDP	20.7	21.3	21.4	22.4	23.8
Domestic expenditure/GDP	18.5	19.0	18.8	20.7	23.1
Tax revenue/GDP	17.9	19.2	19.6	21.5	21.8
Primary balance/GDP	2.1	2.3	2.5	1.7	0.7
Overall balance/GDP	–5.3	–3.3	–3.4	–1.7	–3.2
Net domestic financing/GDP	4.9	0.0	–0.004	–2.2	0.5
End of year inflation %	15.2	9.0	23.6	10.0	11.8

Source: Compiled from Bank of Ghana, Statistical Bulletins

of hardware or infrastructural benefits or from the software perspective, namely, improvements in quality and coverage in service delivery. The strategy prioritised some projects for immediate execution. Notable among these were the construction of feeder roads, the West Africa Gas Pipeline project, modernisation of agriculture via irrigation and storage facilities, agro-processing and establishment of agri-business zones. Under human resource and provision of basic services, education, health and water and sanitation received the most attention, re-echoing the HIPC priorities. The 2003 APR presented achievements to that date on the GPRS targets.

For instance, the government proposed under the education component to establish one model secondary school in each district. A total of 48 billion new cedi (¢) were disbursed for the model senior secondary schools in 2003. There was a significant increase in the gross primary enrolment rate (GPER) in the three deprived northern regions. The GPER in the Upper West Region increased by 6.5 per cent from 63.1 per cent in the 2001/2002 academic year to 69.6 per cent in the 2002/2003, exceeding the GPRS target. For health, the main activity was to abolish the 'cash-and-carry' system and replace it with a health-insurance scheme. Although the scheme was launched in March 2004 and a registration exercise begun, there were several newspaper reports about the considerable difficulty experienced in getting the scheme off the ground, largely as a result of poor management in districts. It is also likely that financial commitments were too low.

Community water and sanitation received a large boost from an acceleration of the provision of rural water through HIPC support. To improve access to safe water in rural and peri-urban communities, with emphasis on guinea-worm endemic areas, 1,290 new boreholes were constructed, 115 boreholes were rehabilitated, 61 new hand dug wells were constructed and 65 small community/town pipe systems were completed. It may be observed, however, that water charges have gone up considerably, particularly for poor urban households without access to their own domestic connections who have to pay for each bucket of water fetched from neighbouring houses. Together with those who pay for truck deliveries, such households were reported to be paying about 65 per cent more for water than other households.

Under governance, the priorities included providing logistics and increasing the police force; the passing of the Local Government Service Bill and the National Procurement Code Bill; and establishing an ad hoc committee on poverty in parliament. Several activities were ongoing at the time of the report that were intended to improve the general framework for safeguarding freedoms as well as promoting transparency, accountability and safety in the country. Capacity development is being carried out in the police force in the form of recruitment and training, new equipment and expansion in coverage of services. In the meantime, the Local Government Service Bill and the Procurement Bill have both been promulgated into law. A Ghana anti-corruption coalition has also been formed to stamp out corruption.

For vulnerable and excluded groups, the GPRS proposes to improve the quality of life of people living with HIV/AIDS, orphans and the physically handicapped, as well as improving services for women and children. The Women and Juvenile Unit of the Ghana Police Force is benefiting from several training programmes to prepare staff for the task of handling victims of domestic violence and child abuse in general. HIV/AIDS has created a new category of vulnerability in the country, and Ghana has embarked on an AIDS treatment project. At the time of writing, only 2,000 people living with HIV/AIDS (PLWHAS) could be supported on the programme, out of an estimated 29,000 who needed treatment.

Irrigation had improved only slightly for the period of the GPRS under examination, expanding by an additional 1,200 hectares of land. This was a very modest step given the central importance of improved irrigation in the agriculture sector. Indeed, it is clear that not much structural change will be forthcoming without a major transformation of agriculture, and irrigation is central to that process. In the roads sector, marked improvement was recorded in the routine and periodic maintenance of feeder roads, achieving 88.8 per cent of targets in 2003 compared to 53.8 per cent in 2002.

In terms of the ultimate objective of poverty reduction, however, the evidence of the report is mixed. According to the GLSS3 and GLSS4 household surveys, the national incidence of poverty fell significantly between 1991/1992 and 1998/1999. The CWIQ1997 and CWIQ 2003 surveys, as well as recent data on macroeconomic trends, seemed to confirm the overall trends reported in the GLSS3 and GLSS4. However, statistical analyses show that the decline in poverty has been concentrated in specific localities (Accra and the rural forest region) and also within particular economic activities (notably, export-oriented sectors and commerce). Similarly, there is some evidence to suggest the deepening of poverty in the northern savannah regions (Coulombe and McKay, 2004).

A new GPRS

Around the time of this study, and after nearly three years experience with implementing the GPRS, the Government of Ghana began developing a new GPRS for the period ahead. This was an important opportunity to learn from any weaknesses in process and content from the initial GPRS. The NDPC expected to produce a consultation document by the end of June 2005. (In fact the document was not ready then, but was expected to be out within a few weeks of the completion of the Ghana country report). It is important to underscore the fact that in the exercise of putting together an update, the process of consultation was quite similar to the first. The use of cross-sectoral planning groups (CSPGs) was maintained and the thematic areas were reduced to give the document a sharper focus. Thus, in the update, the discussion of 'macroeconomy' and 'production and gainful employment' were merged to generate synergy. Environment and gender, as cross-cutting issues, are also strongly emphasised. A validation workshop on the first full draft was held at Sogakope on 30 April 2005 and regional and district consultations began May 2005. In discussions with the NDPC, we observed the strong intent to merge the GPRS with the CPESD, thus solving the problem of possible duplication and also strengthening parliamentary accountability.

IV Quality of the GPRS and its implementation

This section seeks to answer a set of key questions about the nature and quality of the GPRS process. We focus on the whole process – including GPRS documents, the process of drawing them up, strategy implementation and including the link with budget and other government processes – not just on the GPRS documents themselves.

Ownership

A central question is how far the GPRS is seen and accepted – by the Ghana's government, parliament and other country stakeholders – as a country-owned and country-driven strategy? Or is it seen as just another requirement for qualifying for external assistance? Different stakeholders were found to have different perceptions, and in this section we seek to explain reasons for the differences.

ISSER (2005) argues that the process of developing the GPRS and the results of the process are generally perceived to be satisfactory. It notes, however, that while extensive consultations were held prior to the issuing of the document, these were generally among selected bureaucrats, CSOs and donors. In its study, the ISSER observes that many stakeholders believe that consultations should have been extended to local government bodies in a more structured way (as required by the constitution) and also to other members of society in order to foster ownership. Only 12 out of 110 districts were consulted on a draft document. ISSER (2005) observes from fieldwork material that:

> 'At downstream levels there is less confidence about the success of the participatory process. ... respondents selected from elite and non-elite groups[1] in focus-group discussions held in all ten regions of Ghana indicate lower levels of awareness and consultation, especially among the non-elite groups compared to the elite group. For example, non-elite respondents from Eastern and Central Region reported little or no knowledge of the GPRS, let alone make some input. They generally blamed decentralisation problems such as dormant unit committees, assembly members' inability to report to communities and poorly organised durbars for GPRS dissemination as some bottlenecks hampering the GPRS participatory process.'

Table 3.2, below, captures the types of consultation undertaken in relation to the initial GPRS.

In our own discussions with stakeholders, we observed a strong perception that the initial GPRS was developed in haste for PRGF and HIPC purposes. We also found the perception that development partners, including the IFIs, played a particularly strong role at a late stage in the process when priorities were being set.

Within government, there was initially little involvement of sector ministries – their involvement was often described as limited to one or two persons representing the institution at meetings to discuss documents already prepared and not having been previously discussed at the ministry, department or agency. At the same time, while many ministries, departments and agencies (MDAs) were invited to attend meetings to discuss their sectors, they themselves were not required to develop arrangements for an internal discussion of the GPRS, leading to initial discrepancies between their own programmes and the GPRS. We observed that as the GPRS developed through progress reports, the sector ministries felt their strategies were fully included – so that by the time of the report there was reasonably strong ownership across government, as well as in the Ministry of Finance and Economic Planning (MoFEP) and the National Development Planning Commission (NDPC).

Turning to participation and ownership outside central government, we have already noted the limited engagement of local government and district assemblies, an important gap since many of the actions have to be delivered at the district level.

Learning from Experience

Table: 3.2 Chronology of early consultations by activity

Activity	Participants	Date
Conceptualisation forum	Cross section of stakeholders on poverty reduction	March 2000
Launching of GPRS process	Cross section of Ghanaian Society	July 2000
Core teams orientation forums	Core teams	August 2000
Community, district and regional consultations	Community groups, district and regional representatives	Oct.–Nov. 2001
Harmonisation	Core teams, CSOs, private sector, development partners	March 2001
Special Forum for Civil Society (as input into the National Economic Dialogue)	Civil society organisations	May 2001
National Economic Dialogue	Cross section of Ghanaian Society	May 2001
Linking GPRS to annual /MTEF budget	MTEF, Budget Division/ Ministry of Finance	June 2001 to date
Presentation on draft GPRS	Development partners	3 July 2001
GPRS instructional workshop for MDAs	MTEF sectional groupings	23–27 July 2001
GPRS consultation workshop	Chief directors, MDAs	2 August 2001
Calls for comment	Divisional directors, MDAs	8 August 2001
GPRS consultation workshop	NGOs and religious bodies	10 August 2001
GPRS consultation workshop	Labour unions and civil society	17 August 2001
GPRS consultation workshop	Policy advocacy groups and think tanks	20 August 2001
Review workshop	Think tanks, research institutions and policy activists	20 August 2001
Calls for comments	Professional bodies & NUGS, NUPS	24 August 2001
Calls for comments	PEF, AGI, GNCCI, NBSSI[2]	24 August 2001
Calls for comments	Core teams for GPRS	24 August 2001
Calls for comments	National Association of Local Governments	24 August 2001
Calls for comments	Gender networks	31 August 2001
Calls for comments	National Association of Local Governments	24 August 2001
GPRS consultation workshop	Women's groups and media	31 August 2001
Consultation and training workshops	Budget officers, Ministry of Finance	4 Sept. 2001
Policy review workshops with MTEF/ Budget Division	Admin. Group A, Economic and Public Safety Groups	17–18 Sept. 2001
Policy review workshops with MTEF/ Budget Division	Social, Infrastructure and Admin. Group B	19–20 Sept. 2001
GPRS/MTEF cross-sectoral meetings	MDAs	October 2001
Policy hearings	MDAs	10–12 Oct. 2001
Retreat	Parliament	25–27 Oct. 2001
Budget hearings	MDAs	29 Oct.–2 Nov. 2001
Finalisation of draft estimates from MDAs	Ministry of Finance	13–18 Nov. 2001
Review of draft estimates	Cabinet	November 2001
Review of budget with GPRS priorities	Parliament	30 Nov. 2001
Regional and district workshops	Regional & district personnel, CSOs, NGOs	June–December 2001
Stakeholders Forum on draft	Cross section of Ghanaian Society	14 March 2002

Source: GPRS document, pp. 9–10

Parliament is formally engaged in the process, but in practice engagement has not been active. As noted above, participation by other stakeholders in the original process of drawing up the GPRS was extensive, but carried out more on a 'headcount' basis and lacking in substance. The government seemed more anxious to show which civil society organisations participated than in the substance of their participation. Some civil society organisations indicated that they did not have enough time to consider the proposals that were discussed. All commented on the inadequate level of consultation on the macroeconomic framework. Neither did the private sector have much engagement in the process. There were also some doubts about whether enough time and space had been left for more effective consultation on the GPRS that was in preparation in 2005. The effectiveness of the National Economic Dialogue process for generating participation requires some more thinking through.

Other studies[3] have also noted similar shortcomings, summarised below:

- The short GPRS timetable limited the depth and breath of consultation and participation
- The preconceived ideas of the core team dominated decision-making, at the expense of grassroots opinion
- There was a desire to achieve particular outcomes that would satisfy donors
- There was a general lack of active involvement of parliament
- There were difficulties in co-ordinating the MDAs' involvement

While the 2005 GPRS provided an opportunity to address these shortcomings in the consultation process, it is not obvious that the opportunity was properly utilised. We stress, in particular, the need for more engagement with the private sector, including small businesses (and including agriculture), and with local government. More broadly, there is more to be done to develop a national consensus on the approach to development and poverty reduction – and this will require explicit political leadership and endorsement of the new GPRS from the top. There is still a widespread impression that the first GPRS was 'written' in Washington. Indeed, there has been concern that the document presented by the minister to parliament for approval had had far too much influence from the World Bank and the IMF. In our discussions with development partners, some indicated that they were seeking to stand back to give the government more space to make its own decisions. At the same time, recent changes in Washington procedures should help reduce the impression that the strategy needs to be 'approved' by the World Bank and IMF boards. Despite this, we observed from comments at our validation workshop to discuss the initial draft of the report that there was still a strong perception that the process of updating the GPRS was suffering from the earlier haste after a late start to the process. As noted earlier, consultation with selected local government bodies took place after a draft had been completed, and this did not reflect adequately the bottom-up process envisaged in the planning laws. The level of consultation with MDAs also attracted criticism, as did the engagement with civil society and the private sector. It was not so much a question of whether they were invited to meetings or not; it was more a question of how adequately prepared all parties were to engage in fruitful discussions on what the contents of the document should be. The consensus appeared to be that little time was left for that, leaving all the parties poorly prepared. The availability of data to all parties was also questioned.

A point worth noting from the various consultations that were documented on the GPRS was the frequent claim by several groups of stakeholders that they were neither consulted during the preparation of the GPRS nor had they seen the document. The best illustration of this was when a Minister of State said at a meeting of parliament's Appointments Committee that she had not seen the GPRS document. The NDPC responds that consultation was quite wide, which is indeed true. However, it was not wide enough to reach every part of Ghana. It would be desirable to expand outreach and education across the country in order to make all Ghanaians familiar with the contents of the strategy. Getting civic education groups to discuss the document is essential.

National framework or a basis for accountability to development partners?

Underlying many of the issues discussed above is the question: is Ghana's Poverty Reduction Strategy primarily a national framework for guiding policy action, or is it first and foremost an instrument of accountability to the BWIs and other development partners? All those we consulted – government, civil society and donors alike – were clear that the GPRS should be a national document, for which the government is nationally accountable. Donors, however, as well as others were very much aware of the risks of accountability being more to development partners than to a domestic audience, with domestic accountability mechanisms relatively weak and the MDBS group providing a vigorous forum for external accountability. In this context, there was broad support, including from development partners, for efforts to strengthen domestic accountability and the role of parliament in particular. Civil society organisations could play an important role here, interacting with parliament and providing parliamentarians with the material and assistance they need to exercise their oversight role. One donor told us he hoped to see the day when donors would first learn of government policy decisions when sitting in the public gallery of parliament – a hope that we share.

An important related issue is the role of the National Development Planning Commission in preparing the GPRS and monitoring implementation. In discussions during the Ghana study, concerns were expressed about the position of NDPC within government, and the quality of its permanent staff and heavy reliance on consultants. If the GPRS is accepted as a central function of government, providing a framework of accountability to parliament and people, then the process needs strong political leadership and very close integration (as discussed below) with the medium-term and annual budget process. This suggests the need for some repositioning of the NDPC and its work within government, to achieve a closer link with MoFEP on the one hand and on the other, stronger and more active political sponsorship of its work, and the GPRS process, in cabinet and at the highest level. It was strongly suggested during consultations that the MoFEP should be more closely involved in economic management, with a stronger analytical role complementing the strategic thinking role assigned to the NDPC. This means that the Policy Analysis Division of MoFEP needs considerable strengthening in order to backstop the GPRS process, at the same time that NDPC is strengthened with the requisite technical skills for undertaking strategic planning. Equally important is the need for government to signal its commitment to the work of NDPC by according it a higher status in the decision-making arrangements of the state and ensuring it has staff of sufficiently high quality. It is also necessary that the documents of the Commission receive greater attention in cabinet. These are important in showing that commitment to GPRS is total and not just a way of meeting donor requirements.

Nature and quality of the GPRS: what improvements have been made and what further improvements could there be?

The GPRS seeks to address problems that most Ghanaians can identify with. That makes its goals relevant. Indeed, the five areas that were selected for increased policy focus and public expenditures have not been much contested. As was earlier indicated, what has often been raised is the issue of whether adequate emphasis was placed on accelerating growth as an important precondition for poverty reduction. There is no doubt that considerable emphasis was placed on macroeconomic stability. The question is more: was enough made of the possibilities of generating more rapid growth based on a more stable regime? While the GPRS mentions 'production and gainful employment' there is very little by way of a clear policy framework towards achieving that. Indeed, many donors complained of the initial GPRS strategy document being a shopping list that failed to associate particular outcomes with the proposed policy/project interventions.

We thought this a valid criticism, and hoped that without losing the progress made in focusing more attention on key social investments in health, education, water and establishing a poverty monitoring system, the 2005 GPRS would give more attention to policy actions needed to strengthen growth. We believe stronger involvement of the private sector in drawing up the strategy is going to help. This report also highlights that key policy components are likely to include improving the climate for doing business, modernising relevant laws and removing unnecessary regulations on businesses, providing the basic infrastructure needed – roads, port facilities and irrigation – and acting to strengthen the financial sector to make more finance available – especially to small businesses.

In the long term, the key issue is how to get over the various structural bottlenecks to doing business in Ghana. Attention will have to be focused on using public policy and institutions to facilitate the functioning of markets, including financial, land and labour markets. It is worth pointing to the fact that in a number of recent studies on the economy of Ghana and pro-poor growth (Aryeetey and McKay, 2004) emphasis has been placed on enhancing economic management with a view to achieving the synergies that are inherent in the relationship between the public and the private sectors. This is also emphasised in the study by Booth et al (2004) on the 'drivers of change' in Ghana.

In addressing some of the issues above, we note that in the 2005 GPRS the focus on growth led to greater attention to private-sector development. For many of the stakeholders, a key issue was how best to bring down interest rates from well above an average of 25 per cent to manageable levels. Noting that the Bank of Ghana's prime rate had come down somewhat at the time of writing, hitting 16.5 per cent in May 2005 from 18 per cent, the issue remained what it would take to bring the general level of rates down further and bank lending rates closer to the prime rate. This is tied to the maintenance of fiscal responsibility, even as public expenditures must expand in order to deal with large-scale poverty. While some stakeholders called for public policy in allocating credit to small borrowers, there were indications that removing the structural constraints to the operations of financial institutions would be of immense help in getting credit to small and micro-enterprises. Beyond the issue of credit, however, there are several other structural constraints that need to be tackled in order to facilitate private enterprise growth, including entrepreneurship development.

How well is the strategy being implemented?

There is a growing awareness both in government and among development partners that however good the strategy document is, and however well conducted the preparation process, it is worthless unless it is implemented effectively. This recognition – that it is the whole PRS 'process' that matters much more than the PRSP itself (however well written) – is welcome. The process encompasses or should encompass links with sector strategies and action plans, the annual PRS reviews, agreement each year on a policy assessment framework (PAF) and revised medium-term expenditure framework, the annual budget process, and also implementation and results achieved on the ground.

Here, as noted in section II, we see grounds for concern about apparent disconnects between the GPRS and the MTEF, and between the MTEF, the MTP and the budget. Underlying these are concerns about the quality of basic budget and financial management. As discussed in section V below, some of the problems are the result of donor practices. However, it will also take focused government efforts to address them. Many stakeholders were concerned about what they saw to be an uncertain link between the budget and the GPRS activities or programmes, and some identified errors in budget arithmetic designed to demonstrate the link. For a number of reasons, it was difficult to track through from GPRS to decisions set out in the MTEF, MTP or the budget, and some have claimed to find little relationship. Meanwhile, there is a perhaps even more serious concern about uncertainty between budgetary items and actual expenditures on poverty-reduction items. Killick (2004) reports that actual expenditures in health and education deviated markedly from the approved budget. This is attributable partially to other inflows that were not recorded in the budget, largely from donors under sector-wide approaches (SWAps). However, the difference between what was actually spent from government sources and the budget was also quite sizeable, which was attributed to substantial leakages from the system as a result of poor financial management. This situation arose in spite of several attempts to overhaul the system of financial management with assistance from donors.

A World Bank review of public expenditure management identifies the issues that need to be addressed, and suggests a number of important reforms. The first problem is that the budget is highly fragmented and incomplete. Expenditure financed by HIPC debt relief, a number of statutory funds and departmental internally generated funds are outside the budget altogether. We recognise new efforts are being made to address this problem. In addition, despite efforts to improve reporting, many donor project grants remain outside the budget; and expenditure on personnel emoluments is protected. The result is that around 60 per cent of primary public expenditure is not subject to the normal discipline of annual budget decisions, and around 50 per cent falls outside the consolidated fund. A second problem is that the budget is set out in a manner – with much detail and largely activity based – that makes it hard to assess links with the programme priorities set out in the GPRS. The MTEF, which might be expected to provide a link between the GPRS and the budget, has similar shortcomings. It excludes around 60 per cent of primary spending. And while it provides a high level of detail – running to several volumes – it does not group spending into programmes, so it is hard to track the relation with programme priorities as set out in the GPRS.

The final challenge in the public financial management system is to implement better auditing and tracking systems to ensure that budget allocations are used effectively, and reach the front line services they are intended to fund.

Addressing these challenges effectively is a crucial element of creating an effective PRS system and achieving growth and poverty reduction in Ghana. In addition to actions by government, it will require a number of changes by development partners – discussed in the next section – either to move away from project finance or to ensure that their project spending is fully integrated and reported in the national and sectoral budgets. The government recognises the changes that need to be implemented. Recent legislation – the Financial Administration Act, Internal Audit Act and Public Procurement Act – gives the government the powers it needs – for example, to collect project-spending information from development partners; however, that legislation needs to be implemented. Similarly, the new computer-based financial management system (BPEMS), when rolled out, has the potential to produce the right kind of programme-based expenditure forecasts and outturns – but it will be important to use it to do so.

There are other key issues relating to the annual budget process that will need to be addressed if the GPRS strategy is to be implemented more effectively. First, it is important to strengthen the link between the GPRS and annual progress reviews (APR), and the annual performance assessment framework (PAF) negotiated with the IMF and MDBS group of donors. Ideally, the PAF should derive directly from the APR – indeed the two documents might be merged. If they are, it will give the right signal about the appropriate status of the PAF: it should be seen as a statement of government commitment to policy action over the year ahead, and should perhaps be presented to parliament as such, not as a negotiated document.

Second, there is a need, as the government recognises, to greatly strengthen economic management capacity at the MoFEP and national statistical office. The government needs to be able to make its own calculations and forecasts of GDP and growth, revenues and expenditures – rather than rely on the IMF as it does at present – and so determine the fiscal parameters for annual budget decisions. This is unlikely to be achieved without raising pay levels for professional staff sufficiently to recruit individuals for the MoFEP and statistical service with the right levels of competence.

In summary, we believe an effective 'GPRS system' should include the following elements:

- A PAF that relates directly to the GPRS and APR, seen as a statement of government policy intent, rather than as a document negotiated with donors.
- An MTEF and an MTP that includes all relevant expenditure, including donor-financed projects, showing expenditure by programmes aligned with the GPRS.
- Sufficient macroeconomic management capacity at the MoFEP and elsewhere for the government to make its own decisions about the macroeconomic constraints affecting budget decisions.
- An annual budget that also includes all relevant expenditure, again showing expenditure proposals and outturns by programme, aligned with the MTEF and GPRS.
- Arrangements for auditing and tracking to ensure that spending is productive and reaches the front line services for which it is intended.
- A logical annual sequence of decision taking, starting with the GPRS annual progress report, leading to a revised MTEF, with the first year of the MTEF set

out in more detail in the annual budget proposals. The process should run throughout the year.

V Quality of support given by development partners

This section assesses the support being given to Ghana by development partners – both multilateral organisations and bilateral partners. Have they given appropriate support to the PRS process, while leaving the government the space it needs to set national priorities? Have partners acted to align their support behind the priorities set out in the GPRS? Are they moving to improve the effectiveness of their support, reducing administrative demands on government and implementing global agreements to harmonise donor procedures and practices?

Support for preparation and review of the GPRS

For the most part, external support for the GPRS process has been appropriate, both for the original GPRS and the one in preparation at the time of the present study. By this we mean that for the most part external partners appeared to be ready to stand back and let the government set its own priorities for growth and poverty reduction, giving advice and support when asked; and that in general advice when given – as in the IMF/World Bank Joint Staff Assessments (JSAs) of the GPRS and annual progress reports – has been on target.

However, practice has evolved over time, and there are differences between practice at the sectoral level and experience with the GPRS itself. In retrospect, it seems clear that the priorities adopted in 2003, with heavy emphasis on social-sector spending in education and health (and much less emphasis on support for private-sector development, including agriculture, infrastructure or for areas such as social housing) closely reflected what were seen as donor priories at the time and actions seen as necessary to secure HIPC debt relief. With successive annual progress reports and the preparation of the 2005 GPRS, a more balanced set of priorities began to emerge; partners also stood back much more – providing finance for technical assistance but limiting, if not totally avoiding, involvement in policy debate.

To some degree there was a similar evolution with respect to sectoral strategies. In education, for example, as the government has developed and adopted its own education sector strategy it has been able to move from a situation where partners were largely setting the agenda to one where the government sees itself as setting the agenda, and having considerable, if not yet complete, success in persuading donors to support government priorities.

Nonetheless, **we draw attention to a range of more specific points, including some comments on individual partners.** The World Bank has rightly pointed to the need for the Government of Ghana to strengthen its budgeting and public expenditure and financial management systems as critical, but has also tried to stand back, to give the government space to set its own objectives in the GPRS, and has encouraged other donors to do the same. It has helped that the Bank local office is resourced to make a substantial contribution in supporting the process and to be influential in determining the scale and nature of the Bank's support.

The IMF has been trying to strengthen the capacity of the Ministry of Finance and Economic Planning to set its own macro framework. There is the concern, however, that current arrangements by which IMF staff take responsibility themselves for carrying out the calculations and financial programming exercise, rather than insisting that the MoFEP takes on this responsibility itself, may undermine the efforts to achieve significant ownership. There are clearly only very limited numbers of professional staff at the MoFEP with the necessary technical capacity. This can and must be addressed by recruitment and training – and by more effectively using and developing those staff who have received training, for example at IMF-run courses in Washington. A general perception that the quality of external consultation on the macro framework has been significantly lower than in other policy areas could also reflect a relative weakness of government capacity in this area. The very small size of the local IMF office, and its dependence on backup from Washington, has limited its ability to interact locally, though the office does all that is possible with the resources available.

Other partners, including the UNDP and several bilateral donors, have been providing significant technical support for the process – indeed without this it is hard to see how the NDPC, which is poorly resourced, could do its job of producing the GPRS. However, as noted above, this is a second best substitute for strengthening the permanent capacity of the NDPC.

At the sectoral level, where GPRS priorities are linked with detailed sector action plans, partner involvements were found to be rather close. The Ministry of Education and Sports, for example, has general co-ordination meetings with donors every two months, and monthly meetings with donors of four separate thematic groups. Where partner inputs provide useful technical support – for example, providing information about approaches that work in other countries – this can be helpful. However, while progress is being made in the right direction, not all partners yet accept that there is a single national education strategy that they support. While some are prepared to support the strategy, either with finance channelled through the budget or through the education basket fund, others still seek to impose their own priorities by offering funds that are earmarked or to be channelled to individual projects that would not otherwise be on the government's priority list.

Despite the general growing willingness of partners to give the government the space it needs to make its own decisions in the GPRS, and the clear adoption of the GPRS as the present government's central medium-term strategy for growth and poverty reduction as mentioned above, the perception persists that the strategy in some sense has to be approved in Washington. Indeed, we were told that the initial GPRS was presented to parliament as a strategy already 'approved' by the boards of the World Bank and IMF. In our view, this is not appropriate for the government's central development strategy document, which should be approved by government and parliament, not by the boards of the Bank and the IMF (although clearly the boards need to assess the level and nature of support they are prepared to give). We hope that recent changes in procedures for considering country PRSs in the boards of the Bank and the IMF removed any impression that the 2005 GPRS had to be 'approved' in Washington.

Alignment of support from development partners

Has financial support from the IMF and the World Bank – e.g. through the Poverty Reduction Growth Facility (PRGF) and Poverty Reduction Support Credits (PRSCs) – been grounded as intended in the GPRS? And have other partners and donors accepted the PRS and sector strategies as the basis for their continued financial support? In this context, we see the development of the Multi-Donor Budget Support programme (MDBS) as particularly encouraging, providing assistance from development partners to finance budgetary operations over the medium-term in support of the GPRS. MDBS represents a shift from a sectoral- and project-driven approach to a more long-term development partnership based on budget support. Ten development partners are involved in a memorandum of understanding with the Government of Ghana: the African Development Bank, Canada, Denmark, Germany, the European Union, France, the Netherlands, Switzerland, the UK and the World Bank. Budget support with funding commitments from development partners totalling 232.6 million euros was given in the first year of operation (2003).

The benefits of the MDBS, as seen by the Government of Ghana, are the reduction of transaction costs associated with official development assistance (ODA), including those transaction costs arising from meeting multiple conditions attached by different donors to flows of ODA; increased predictability of ODA flows, allowing for better long-term planning; increased institutional capability; increased democratic accountability to its electorate; institutionalised strategic policy dialogue; and increased local ownership of the programme since the GPRS represents a government-led process and document. MDBS is the key tool for supporting the implementation of the GPRS, by strengthening the institutional environment within the GPRS mandate and by emphasising the importance of public financial management, public sector reforms and governance issues. The support is staggered in two tranches; the first tranche (base payment) is payable following a positive IMF review and the payment of the second tranche (performance payment) depends on the outcome of a progress assessment on five key areas of reform: public financial management, the budget process, decentralisation, public sector reform and governance. (It is of interest that remaining direct donor funding to sectors was less consistent with the GPRS than budget spending by the Government of Ghana). In 2002, donor sectoral allocation of resources decreased in both the administration and economic sectors. Social services and infrastructure resources were increased, while agriculture resource allocation decreased. The increase in social services as a whole did not include education (which decreased by 0.1 per cent), but the health sector had a substantial increase from 4.9 per cent to 8 per cent in 2002.

That said, we believe that most donors, particularly those giving budget/sector support, appear to have been trying to take the government's policies and priorities set out in the GPRS and sector strategies as the basis for their support; nonetheless, we think there are several issues that will need attention in future.

While the macro frameworks in the GPRS and the annual progress reports are reasonably well aligned with those in the PRGF, this is at least in part because, as noted above, the government has in practice left it to IMF staff to take a lead role in the construction of the macro programme in both documents. Like other GPRS processes, the government's macroeconomic strategy should be – and should be seen to be – government-led, with government accountability to parliament and people (and not to the IMF). As is also noted above, achieving this will require a significant strengthening of the government's macroeconomic management and related statistical capacity.

The trend towards budget or sector-wide support is clearly helping align support better with government strategies. At the level of the overall budget, the MDBS policy assessment framework (PAF), which also acts as a framework for the World Bank's PRSC, is partly but not wholly grounded in the GPRS. Moreover, the MoFEP expresses strong ownership of the measures set out in the PAF. Pressures from some donors to add a number of specific conditions from outside the GPRS framework are being resisted by other donors. However, we suggest that it would help presentationally if the PAF was presented not as a document negotiated with partners, but as a simple statement of government policy derived from the GPRS and setting out objectives and targets in more detail – perhaps as part of the GPRS/APR – with the MDBS group of donors indicating which actions they would take as triggers. At present, the PAF has the appearance to some of being a negotiated document listing a set of donor imposed 'conditions'.

The trend to financial support through the MDBS or in sector support through SWAps has also in practice helped increase the predictability of aid flows. Compared with significant shortfalls against commitments in earlier years, MDBS donors disbursed 100 per cent of their commitments over the two years preceding the report, and most of them are in practice making multi-year commitments. Donors still largely follow their own domestic budget cycles, however, but suggest that they are working on changing this to coincide with the Ghana budget cycle where feasible.

Hopes that the move to budget and sector support will reduce transactions costs have not so far been realised. As discussed further below, the work of the MDBS group of donors, and individual sector groups as well, is backed by an extensive system of donor working groups, each of which places considerable demands on the time of sector ministries. And although the government has imposed some discipline by insisting on joint sessions between the MDBS group and the IMF and MoFEP, working to the ministry's timetable, the group continues to place considerable demands on the time of MoFEP officials. There is, of course, a natural tension here, with both sides accepting the need for sufficiently frequent and intense contact to establish mutual trust between government and development partners. Over time, it should be possible to maintain an adequate level of trust with less frequent and time-consuming meetings.

At the sector level, however, as discussed above, the perception in government at least is that some partners providing support for sector funding baskets seem to be less willing to simply follow the government's lead, seeking to influence or change sector strategies by earmarking funds.

We have even greater concerns about the continued support provided by nearly all partners for individual projects, including support from those – the US (including the Millennium Challenge Corporation [MCC]) and Japan – who remain reluctant to provide budget or sector-wide support and remain observer members only of the MDBS. It is by no means clear that all projects supported fall within government priorities as set out in the GPRS, central budget documents and sector strategies. The MCC is negotiating a programme of support with the government, so when agreed it will also be agreed by the government, but the resulting financial flows – like other US aid – will fall outside the government's budget framework, unless steps are taken (as proposed below) to ensure that they are included. Another example quoted to us during this research was a recent proposal from the World Bank Group for a micro-, small and medium enterprise (MSME) project separate from the set of agreed policies supporting this sector set out in the PAF: the question asked was why could the World Bank not simply increase its support through the budget for the set of policies already set out in the PAF? In any event, it will be important for the government to ensure that all projects supported by the MCC, World Bank and other donors fall clearly within its GPRS priorities. In general, we feel that the government could and should take a stronger stand to ensure that where donors prefer to support individual projects, all such projects are within the government's programme and priorities, and in line with GPRS priorities. On occasion, the government should be prepared to say 'no'.

As discussed in section III, it is problematic for sector ministries and the MoFEP to capture and reflect donor expenditure in support of projects and sector strategies in their tracking of implementation of the GPRS, and it will take action by donors as well as government to address this. For the MoFEP, the current fragmented and weak national budgeting and financial management system – with only some 60 per cent of primary spending subject to adjustment in the budget process – is at least in part a result of partner demands for separate funds for individual purposes. The continued emphasis by some donors on providing support direct to individual projects with separate accounting and auditing arrangements adds a further level of complexity to the task of tracking and accounting for overall progress in implementing GPRS policies. At a minimum, all planned and actual donor project outlays should be promptly reported to government, so they can be included in sector and overall expenditure planning and monitoring.

Could Ghana use an increase in donor financing for the MDGs effectively?

Aid flows to Ghana have been increasing substantially in recent years, and there is a good prospect of further increases in future so long as policy reform continues on track. Indeed recent debt relief announcements show Ghana as a major recipient of new assistance. We believe that with the further improvements in the GPRS process – especially financial management, attention to service delivery on the ground and improved modalities for support by development partners – Ghana will be able to make effective use of steadily increasing aid flows over the years ahead.

The Multi-Donor Budget Support (MDBS) programme arrangements, in particular, provide a good framework for a substantial scaling up of aid, and we encourage donors to channel increased resources in this way as far as possible.

However, there are two potential risks to guard against. First, there is the risk that a substantial increase in aid volumes could bring with it demands for stronger accountability to donors. This makes it all the more important to take steps to strengthen the government's financial management capacity and accountability to parliament and the people, on the lines suggested above – and to insist that donors accept such capacity and accountability as adequate, rather than insisting on separate accountability to them.

Second, there is the concern that a large increase in aid inflows could bring problems of 'Dutch disease', appreciating the real exchange rate and crowding out private activity. This of course is a 'problem' that could result from other forms of foreign exchange inflows also, such as increased remittance flows or increased inward investment. However, it seems unlikely to us that this constitutes a problem – so long as aid flows build steadily, over a period, and are sustained, with action taken to address bottlenecks such as the supply of trained teachers and health workers. Much of the spending

Table 3.3: Net aid from all donors in current millions, US$

Year	Aid (Current Millions, US$)
1980	192
1987	413
1988	577
1989	718
1990	563
1991	882
1992	615
1993	624
1994	548
1995	651
1996	651
1997	494
1998	702
1999	609
2000	600
2001	653
2002	653
2003	565
2004	709

Source: African Development Bank, African Development Indicators

financed by extra aid will result directly or indirectly in increased imports – and in any event, at the margin non-price factors such as quality and access to markets are likely to be more important than price in determining the competitiveness of Ghanaian products.

Donor co-ordination and harmonisation of practices and procedures

How well is the process of donor co-ordination and harmonisation working? It is clear that in the past development partners imposed major costs on the Ghanaian government, with demands on the time of key officials and practices and procedures that have complicated – and probably to some degree undermined – financial management. It is an indicator of how much MoFEP officials' time is spent handling relations with partners that the ministry has had to appoint an individual 'desk officer' for each partner. For the key sector ministries too, as already illustrated, there are severe demands on the time of key officials from complex sector donor co-ordination arrangements. Meanwhile, at the national level, there are now quarterly 'mini' consultative group meetings as well as regular meetings of the MDBS group of partners, with parallel regular meetings of MDBS sector groups.

It is clear that better donor co-ordination and harmonisation could make a major contribution to strengthening government capacity, by reducing unnecessary demands, and also to strengthening government systems. Efforts are already being made by some partners in this respect, particularly those engaged on the MDBS group. Nonetheless, there is a large agenda, with much to be done, and it would help if – as in some other countries – the government itself were to take a stronger lead in driving change in donor behaviour.

A key element, as discussed in section III, has to be reform of the budget planning, and financial management and control systems. Recent analysis and advice by the World Bank indicates what is needed, but reform will require changes on the part of partners also.

The trend towards channelling more support through budget support or sector baskets will help, but substantial flows in direct support to projects will remain. The World Bank, for example, envisages moving to channelling around 40 per cent of its support through the budget in PRSCs, but the remainder will flow to other projects or as technical assistance. It is important to move to a situation where all continuing support to individual projects is properly included in the budget envelope, and if possible accounted for within normal government systems – cutting out parallel systems.

All members of the MDBS, including the World Bank and IMF, have agreed to a timetable that involves joint missions, a critical point in the process and this appears to be working well. However, those engaged in the MDBS group believe that initially it may have increased rather than reduced transactions costs. To some extent, this reflects a period in which trust is being built on both sides – in the predictability of donor budget support, and in the strengthening of government budgeting and accounting procedures. Over time, it will be important to act to reduce these costs by reducing the number and frequency of MDBS and sector group meetings. Other important donor actions to reduce transaction costs include acceptance within the MDBS group of 'lead agencies' on different issues; and the trend in many donors to decentralise decision taking to local offices.

We believe the time may have come for the Government of Ghana to give a stronger lead to all these efforts: increasing awareness across all ministries of the global agenda for better alignment and harmonisation of donor procedures and practices; holding partners in Ghana to the global commitments they have made and setting out an agreed programme of change; and instituting a system for monitoring compliance and implementation by partners (for example, by reporting numbers of missions, percentage of projects captured in budget documents and so on).

V   Main findings and recommendations

Successes and areas for attention in the Ghana PRS process

Developing and implementing the Ghana Poverty Reduction Strategy was a learning process, and the second GPRS, launched summer 2005, benefited from these lessons. As GPRS II was developed and implemented, it was also important to continue to learn from the experience of implementing GPRS I. Recognising that in most cases relevant improvements were already under way at the time of writing, we find scope for such improvement in six areas.

Establishing full national ownership of the GPRS process

Fully integrating the GPRS into the national policy framework proved a difficult and continuing task, partly as a result of the origins of the first GPRS – which was drawn up in some haste and with an emphasis on policies believed to be important to qualify for heavily indebted poor country (HIPC) debt relief. Even with the development of the 2005 GPRS, the process was not yet complete. In this respect, we see a need for action in the areas outlined below.

First, **further steps could be taken to set the strategy more firmly in the context of Ghana's constitution and national political processes.** The Government of Ghana sees the GPRS as its central strategy for development, supplemented by more detailed sectoral strategies, and in that sense there is strong ownership, at least at the centre of government. However, under Ghana's constitution, the government is required to develop and present a 'Co-ordinated Programme for Economic and Social Development' (CPESD), and to use processes in generating development priorities that start at the local level with district development plans – the opposite of processes used in generating both the first and second GPRSs, which have been top down rather than bottom up. A fully nationally owned process might be expected to be based on the national constitution rather than a pattern suggested by the Bretton Woods Institutions. The 2005 GPRS takes a step in this direction, as it was also presented as a new CPESD. However, the process of preparation was still top down, rather than the process envisaged in the constitution and the planning laws, with only minimal engagement of local government and district assemblies. We believe it is not too soon to consider bringing the process for preparing future PRS strategies in Ghana more fully into line with the country's constitutionally mandated political process.

Second, **the content of the GPRS should cover all elements of a national development strategy.** If key elements are missing or given insufficient priority, the strategy is unlikely to succeed. It is also essential for enhancing ownership across government: all ministries and agencies need to feel part of the process. We welcome the emphasis in the 2005 GPRS on economic growth, and the policies and infrastructure needed to promote it, as well as on continued social investment. A clear macroeconomic framework and prioritisation are also essential, not least to ensure continued progress in reducing real and nominal interest rates as an important contribution to growth and investment. We hope this macroeconomic framework can be set out both in the GPRS and in annual progress reports in a way that will provide a basis for more effective dialogue – for example, with civil society and parliament – than was achieved in the first GPRS. We also note that representatives of the private sector feel they had insufficient chance to provide input to the 2005 GPRS, and hope further opportunities can be given as the strategy is developed and implemented.

A third area for action is that **sector ministries and agencies should see their sector strategies as clearly linked to and flowing from the GPRS.** We believe that there has been progress in this direction, but that there is also some way to go. Despite efforts to involve sector ministries more in preparation of the 2005 GPRS, their representatives did not always provide an effective two-way link, and for this and other reasons preparation of the 2005 GPRS was not fully successful in providing the opportunity it should have for rethinking sector strategies.

Strengthening and rationalising the implementation process (as discussed below) will also help embed the PRS process better into the national policy framework, **but it is important for all elements, including policy assessment frameworks and letters of intent to the IMF, to be seen and presented as national policy documents for which the** government is responsible – and not as documents negotiated with or imposed by development partners.

Finally, we see an essential role for parliament in approving the strategy, and holding the government to account for its implementation. Parliament itself needs to build up its capacity to exercise an effective accountability role, and we believe civil society organisations can and should provide much assistance in this respect – devoting as much if not more effort to interacting with parliament as they do to interactions with government and development partners.

Strengthening and rationalising the implementation process

The recognition that it is the whole PRS 'process' that matters much more than the PRSP itself (however well written) is welcome. **Ongoing efforts to strengthen and rationalise public financial management and accountability arrangements in Ghana are therefore central to success – not only in implementing the GPRS, but also in deepening national ownership and establishing an efficient relationship with development partners.** The process encompasses or should encompass: links with sector strategies and action plans; the annual PRS reviews (APRs); agreement each year on a policy assessment framework (PAF), and revised medium-term expenditure framework (MTEF) and MTP; the annual budget process; and also implementation and monitoring of results achieved on the ground. Each of the following elements needs further attention:

- A PAF that relates directly to the GPRS and APR, seen as a statement of government policy intent, rather than as a document negotiated with donors.
- An MTEF that includes all relevant expenditure, including donor-financed projects, showing expenditure by programme aligned with the GPRS.
- Clear government decisions each year on the macroeconomic framework and the macroeconomic constraints affecting budget decisions.
- An annual budget that includes all relevant expenditure, showing expenditure proposals and outturns by programme, aligned with the MTEF and GPRS.
- Arrangements for auditing and tracking to ensure that spending is productive and reaches the front-line services for which it is intended.
- A logical annual sequence of decision-taking, starting with the GPRS APR, leading to a revised MTEF, with the first year of the MTEF set out in more detail in the annual budget proposals.

Enhancing central government capacity

Implementing these changes will require further strengthening of capacity in the MoFEP and NDPC – and probably some consideration of the relative roles and relationships between these two bodies. **At the MoFEP, capacity needs strengthening for both its macroeconomic management and budget management tasks.** The government needs to be able to make its own calculations and forecasts of GDP and growth, revenues and expenditures – rather than rely on the IMF as it does at present – and so determine the fiscal parameters for annual budget decisions. Similarly, it needs a larger and more professional group of staff handling budget preparation, implementation and auditing. In both cases, this means recruiting people with the right skills: in neither case is it satisfactory to rely on external consultants. This is unlikely to be achieved without raising pay levels for professional staff sufficiently so as to be able to recruit individuals for the MoFEP and statistical service with high enough levels of competence.

At the NDPC there is a similar need to upgrade full-time staff and reduce reliance on consultants. In addition, given its central role in the GPRS process, we would like to see the NDPC's role strengthened in two ways. First, ensuring implementation of the GPRS will require increasingly close involvement of the NDPC with the MoFEP, and with PAF, MTEF, budget and other annual financial management processes. Second, given the central national importance of the GPRS, the NDPC may need stronger political leadership both inside and outside government from the highest level in cabinet.

Moving from accountability to development partners to national accountability

Over the years, development partners have established quite elaborate arrangements for ensuring accountability to themselves for the Ghanaian government's development strategies and progress made in implementing policies and projects. Arrangements for continuing policy dialogue with the MDBS group of donors, and also at the sector level, have acted to strengthen such accountability further. To avoid undermining moves to strengthen national accountability, development partners need over time to draw back from these arrangements, and rely more on the government's arrangements for accounting to parliament and people for the country's development strategy and its implementation.

Changes already made in procedures in the BWIs should help to reduce any impression that the GPRS itself has to be 'approved' in Washington. However, we believe partners can do more to remove any impression that the macro framework, or PAF, is 'written in Washington'. Partners should accept that the process is and should be seen to be government led. Meanwhile, the government should publish the relevant documents, including its letters of intent to the IMF, as setting out policies for which the government is responsible and accountable to parliament and people, rather than as texts negotiated with development partners.

As domestic financial management and accountability is strengthened, development partners must be ready to draw back. For example, sector-level meetings should become less frequent, with partners only interacting at key points in the annual policy cycle; and partners must become more willing to accept the government's own regular financial and statistical reports as indicators of progress.

Increasing external support and aligning it better with country priorities

Aid flows to Ghana have been increasing substantially in recent years, and there is a good prospect of further increases in future so long as policy reform continues on track. We believe that with the further improvements in the GPRS process, especially in financial management and attention to service delivery on the ground, and with improvements being made in modalities for support by development partners, **Ghana will be able to make effective use of steadily increasing aid flows over the years ahead.** The MDBS arrangements, in particular, provide a good framework for a substantial scaling up of aid, and we would like to encourage donors to channel increased resources in this way as far as possible.

Most donors, particularly those giving budget/sector support, appear to have been trying to take the government's policies and priorities set out in the GPRS and sector strategies as the basis for their support. Nonetheless, we see several issues that need attention in future. First, while the macro frameworks in the GPRS and annual progress reports are reasonably well aligned with those in the PRGF, this is at least in part because the government has left it to IMF staff to construct the macro programme in both documents. As noted above, we think that like other GPRS processes, the government's macroeconomic strategy should be government-led, with government accountability to parliament and the people (and not to the IMF).

Second, the trend towards budget or sector-wide support is clearly helping align support better with government strategies. If, as we suggest, the PAF was presented not as a document negotiated with partners, but as a simple statement of government policy derived from the GPRS (although setting out objectives and targets in more detail) – perhaps as part of the GPRS/APR – then the MDBS group of donors could indicate which of the proposed actions they would take as benchmarks influencing future levels of support. At present, the PAF has the appearance to some of being a negotiated document listing a set of donor-imposed 'conditions'.

The trend to financial support through the MDBS or in sector support through SWAps has also in practice helped increase the predictability of aid flows. Compared with significant shortfalls against commitments in earlier years, MDBS donors disbursed 100 per cent of their commitments over the two years leading up to the Ghana study. Most such donors are also making multi-year commitments, and we urge others to move swiftly to follow suit. A country like Ghana, which is financing 40 per cent or more of its budget from donor flows, has to have a reasonable assurance of the continuity of such flows.

Finally, at the sector level the perception in government is that some partners providing support for sector funding baskets are not always willing to simply follow the government's lead, seeking rather to influence or change sector strategies by earmarking funds. We have even greater concerns about the continued support provided by nearly all partners for individual projects. It is not clear that all such projects fall within government priorities as set out in the GPRS, central budget documents and sector strategies. In general, we feel that the government could and should take a stronger stand to ensure that where donors prefer to support individual projects, all such projects are within the government's programme and priorities, and in line with GPRS priorities. At the very least, all planned and actual donor project outlays should be promptly reported to government so they can be included in sector and overall expenditure planning and monitoring. On occasion, the government should be prepared to say 'no'.

Implementing commitments by development partners to reduce transaction costs

Development partners can and should do more to reduce strains on government by implementing in Ghana the global commitments they have made on harmonisation and co-ordination of donor practices. Efforts are already being made by some partners in this respect, particularly those engaged on the MDBS group. However, there is a large agenda, with much to be done, and it would help if the government itself were to take a stronger lead in driving change in donor behaviour.

A key element will be reform of budget planning and of financial management and control systems, as noted above. At the same time it is important to move to a situation where all continuing support to individual projects is properly included in the budget envelope, and if possible accounted for within normal government systems – cutting out parallel systems.

All members of the MDBS, including the World Bank and the IMF, have agreed to a timetable that involves joint missions at a critical point in the annual process and this appears to be working well. In other respects, those engaged in the MDBS group believe that initially it may have increased rather than reduced transactions costs. Over time it will be important to act to reduce these costs, for example by reducing the number and frequency of MDBS and sector group meetings. It is also important to continue efforts to reduce the number of visiting donor missions and to establish quiet periods of the year when no missions visit.

Other important donor actions to reduce transaction costs include acceptance within the MDBS group of 'lead agencies' on different issues; and the trend among many donors to decentralise decision-taking to local offices.

The Government of Ghana could give a stronger lead to all these efforts, increasing awareness across ministries of the agreed global agenda for better alignment and harmonisation of donor procedures and practices; holding partners in Ghana to the global commitments they have made and setting out an agreed programme of change; and instituting a system for monitoring compliance and implementation by partners.

The government could also consider implementing periodic independent and transparent reviews of donor practices and progress in implementing a programme of change.

Lessons for other countries and the international community

What lessons do we draw from this study for other countries and the international community? In general, experience with the Poverty Reduction Strategy process in Ghana seems to confirm many of the lessons from elsewhere, in particular:

- The role that respect for pre-existing national processes – in Ghana's case, processes laid down in the constitution and planning laws – can play in enhancing national ownership.
- The need for the strategy to cover all policies relevant to development, including, crucially, policies for promoting growth and private-sector development, as well as social priorities.
- The importance of the whole PRS process, including implementation arrangements. However good a strategy document, it is useless unless implemented effectively.
- The central importance in this respect of establishing good systems of public financial management, including monitoring and evaluation, firmly linked to the PRS.
- The parallel importance of establishing and strengthening arrangements for national accountability to parliament and the people, both for the strategy and its implementation.
- The need for donors to stand back, respect national processes and ensure that where they provide project or sector support it is firmly grounded in country priorities, with spending included and accounted for in national budgets.

- The many benefits of budget or sector-wide support as aid modalities in relation to the traditional project-based approach.

The need for donors to also take a range of actions to reduce transactions costs, and the parallel need for the government to take a lead in holding partners to their global commitments in this respect.

Notes

1. The 'elite' group comprised people who could speak English and are often engaged in formal employment while the 'non-elite' was made up of persons who could neither speak nor write in English.
2. Public Enterprise Foundation, Association of Ghana Industries, Ghana National Chamber of Commerce and Industry and National Board of Small Scale Industry.
3. Killick, T and C Abugre (2001) p. 30.

CHAPTER 4

Monitoring IFI and Donor Support for Poverty Reduction Strategies: Malawi

Chinyamata Chipeta[1] *and David Peretz*

I Introduction

This chapter presents the third of the country reports prepared under the Commonwealth Secretariat project to monitor implementation of the Poverty Reduction Strategy (PRS) process in Commonwealth countries.

In preparing the report, we drew on a number of previous studies and held a first round of discussions in Malawi with representatives of government, the private sector, civil society and development partners, including officials of the IMF and World Bank. We focused on a set of key issues and questions developed as a template for the series of country reports. A preliminary draft report and its preliminary findings and suggestions were discussed at a workshop held in Lilongwe on 7 February 2006. This final report reflects that discussion and also takes account of subsequent developments.

The chapter is organised as follows. Section II describes the Poverty Reduction Strategy (PRS) process as it has evolved and continues to evolve in Malawi, through the period of the first Malawi PRS (MPRS), leading up to preparation of the new Malawi Growth and Development Strategy (MGDS). Section III examines issues to do with the strategy itself and its implementation. Section IV discusses the quality of support being given by development partners. Section V summarises our main findings and recommendations.

II Evolution of the PRS process in Malawi

The Malawi Poverty Reduction Strategy Paper (MPRSP) was developed in the early 2000s at the request of the Bretton Woods Institutions (BWIs) so that the country could benefit from debt relief under the enhanced heavily indebted poor countries (HIPC) initiative, a poverty reduction and growth facility arrangement and other concessionary assistance. The MPRSP has two key elements: a set of government policies and priorities, both overall and for individual sectors; and broad expenditure allocations, covering both domestic and donor funding. Its purpose is to try and ensure that scarce resources are allocated in accordance with government policies and priorities for poverty reduction. In varying degrees, the MPRSP drew upon and learnt from a number of previous national development strategies. The 1987–1996 Statement of Development Policies, which was developed through extensive consultations within government, contained a profile of the poor, the causes of poverty and the measures for addressing the problem of poverty. In the early 1990s, the government started implementing the Social Dimensions of Adjustment Project to minimise the adverse effects of Structural Adjustment Programmes (SAPs) on the poor and strengthen the capacity for integrating the poor in the national development process. In 1995, the government published a policy framework for the Poverty Alleviation Programme, which was developed through an internal consultation process. It identified groups that were considered poor and policies for alleviating poverty.

Vision 2020 followed the Poverty Alleviation Programme in 1998. For the purpose of creating the vision, the Malawi government set up a National Core Team (NCT) comprising ten persons from the private sector, the government and the University of Malawi to manage the process. As it was intended as a shared vision incorporating people's aspirations, the government chose a participatory process to formulate this long-term perspective development strategy. This process included two workshops, a period of wider consultation with Malawians and a national conference to discuss the draft Vision, leading to the final adoption and launch of the Malawi Vision 2020 document.

However, neither the Poverty Alleviation Programme nor Vision 2020 was followed by concrete or fundable action plans. Upon the introduction of the PRSP concept, both the policy framework of the Poverty Alleviation Programme and the Vision 2020 became source documents, although it was observed that no thematic working group used them seriously as inputs into the formulation of the PRSP (Jenkins and Tsoka, 2003). Before preparing a full PRSP, the BWIs requested Malawi to prepare an interim PRSP (I-PRSP). Between them, the National Economic Council and the then Ministry of Finance and Economic Planning prepared the I-PRSP and submitted it in December 2000 to enable an early start to debt relief. Essentially, the I-PRSP was prepared in a hurry without wide consultation outside official circles.

Preparation and content of the MPRSP

The institutional structure that guided the preparation of the Malawi PRSP was dominated by the government. A Technical Committee was set up to manage the process; it was composed of officials from the Ministry of Finance and Economic Planning, the National Economic Council (the chair) and the Reserve Bank of Malawi. It reported to a National Steering Committee comprising principal secretaries from key ministries which, in turn, reported to a Ministerial Committee comprising the Minister of Finance, Director-General of the National Economic Council, the Governor of the Reserve Bank and the Minister of Agriculture (the chair). Broad participation was allowed at the level of developing the MPRSP. The development of sector strategies was given to 21 Thematic Working Groups (TWGs), which were composed of relevant officials/representatives from government, civil society, the private sector, parliamentary committees, statutory bodies, international organisations and donors. The TWGs made submissions to the Technical Committee on the basis of which it drafted the PRSP, along with two representatives of civil society and a representative of a research institution.

The highlights of the consultation process were district workshops, which were facilitated by members of the Technical Committee and some members of the TWGs and held from 5–23 February 2001. The purpose of these workshops was to explain the PRSP process, discuss the government's proposed strategy and to discuss the prioritisation of issues for poverty reduction in the districts. Participants were local members of parliament, councillors, politicians, traditional authorities, local non-governmental organisations and other influential people in the districts. It appears that altogether 1,193 people attended. The gender distribution is not known exactly since most of the district lists did not distinguish between men and women. In the few districts that did so, the number of women ranged from one to six, far below the number of male participants.

The causes of poverty and strategies for addressing them as summarised in the MPRSP can be found in table 4.1, below.

The information in this table is misleading to the extent that it conveys the impression that poverty in Malawi is caused only by factors that constrain the productivity of natural, human and physical capital and of supporting public institutions. The characterisation of the poor and the contents of the poverty-reduction programme in the MPRSP indicate that it is recognised that poverty is also caused by: inadequate use of science and technology; inadequate financial and social capital; unequal distribution of political power; limited market opportunities; and vulnerability to exogenous factors, such as droughts, floods and other natural disasters, and to economic instability, among other things. The main goal of the MPRSP was to achieve sustainable poverty reduction through empowerment of the people. The MPRSP saw the poor as active participants in economic development. It was built around four groups of activities and policies, known as pillars, and a mechanism for monitoring and evaluation:

- **Sustainable pro-poor growth** – economically empowering the poor by ensuring access to credit and markets, skills development and employment generation (Pillar 1).
- **Human capital development** – ensuring that the poor have the health status and education to lift themselves out of poverty (Pillar 2).
- **Improving the quality of life of the most vulnerable** – providing sustainable safety nets for those who are unable to benefit from the first two pillars (Pillar 3).
- **Good governance** – ensuring that public and civil society institutions and systems protect and benefit the poor (Pillar 4). In addition, there are four issues that cut across the four pillars: HIV/AIDS, gender, environment, and science and technology.
- Involvement of all stakeholders in implementation with the Ministry of Finance co-ordinating public expenditure, National Statistical Office co-ordinating all outcomes and impact monitoring across all sectors, and the National Economic Council serving as a focal point for poverty analysis, documentation and dissemination of poverty data.

The Malawi PRS process was described as involving selective participation at the beginning while being broadly open at the end. However, stakeholders raised questions about the selection of those who took part, the commitment of those who were invited to take part and the quality of their participation. They also raised questions about the adequacy of representation of special interest groups and of women, who were marginalised in district consultations. Other problems with the Malawi PRS process relate to the institutional set-up and the time frame. The Technical Committee did not include non-official stakeholders; both that committee and the drafting committee were dominated by economists. The commitment of committee members to the process declined with time, because they were not released for the full time of the exercise. Some of the TWGs lacked technical back-up, so their work suffered. Others were inactive. The quality of

Table 4.1: Causes of poverty and proposed strategies

Causes	Strategies
Land related	
Loss of soil fertility due to rapid environmental degradation	Promote the use of organic fertiliser; distribute free inputs to the most vulnerable
Rapid decrease in land access due to population pressure	Support implementation of the draft land policy; address the problem of small landholding sizes and landlessness through land redistribution, family planning, soil conservation and mechanisation and use of organic fertilisers
Labour related	
Low levels of education	Instil a business culture in smallholder farmers; improve teaching/ working and learning conditions for teachers and pupils, respectively; increase access to education for girls, orphans and children with special needs; increase access to adult literacy classes for those who are out of school; increase access to public secondary schools for all including girls, children with special needs and orphans
General poor health	Provide an essential health care package to all; promote community-based nutrition interventions; strengthen food and nutrition programmes
The devastating effects of the HIV/Aids pandemic	Ensure that pupils and youth have the knowledge and skills to avoid HIV infection and are provided with counselling skills; prevent infection among the general public; improve management of HIV/ AIDS-related conditions; mainstream HIV/AIDS in all sectors and at all planning levels and develop sound support systems for HIV/ AIDS interventions
Lack of or limited off-farm employment	Ensure access to skills development; promote self employment in the informal sector; increase the quality, productivity and marketability of indigenous skills
Rapid population growth	Encourage family planning
Gender inequalities	Conduct gender mainstreaming campaigns in all sectors and at all levels of planning; conduct surveys on gender-based biases in all sectors and social life and then develop policy and programmes to remove gender inequalities
Capital and technology	
Lack of access to credit	Increase access to credit for farmers; reduce base interest rate; expand micro-finance coverage; improve quality of micro-finance supply
Inappropriate technology	Conduct demand-driven research to develop easily adoptable technologies; promote development of local agro-storage and processing industry; increase access to draught animals and animal-drawn implements; increase access to tractor hire; introduce technologies to facilitate income generation
Supporting institutions	
Weak institutional structures	Review and establish realistic and equitable remuneration in the public sector; improve accountability of civil servants for results; establish mechanisms for citizens to hold the civil service accountable for its actions

Learning from Experience

some of the submissions was poor (Tsoka, 2004). From the official launch of the exercise in January 2001, the government wanted the process to be completed in six months. Civil society considered this to be too short a period and so pressed for more time, which was granted. The process dragged on until April 2002 (see table 4.2) as some TWGs were slow. The speed adopted by the Technical Committee affected participation, as meetings were called at short notice. Furthermore, the time extension did not necessarily improve participation.

Integration of the PRSP into the planning and budgeting systems

According to a recent assessment, attempts to integrate the MPRSP into the planning system at ministerial level have been made, but the former has not been fully integrated into the latter (Chirwa, 2005). More specifically, there is in most cases little evidence that the plans of the sectoral ministries are conforming to the MPRSP matrix. Furthermore, ministries do not report on issues that are in the MPRSP matrix, especially if they are not receiving pro-poor expenditures. The study attributed limited penetration of the MPRSP process in sector ministries to capacity constraints.

According to the PRSP, in order to be implemented, the document must be translated into the medium-term expenditure framework (MTEF) and the budget at all levels,

Table 4.2: Chronology of the PRSP process in Malawi

Date	Activity
October 2000	Issuance of Issues Paper by the Technical Committee
December 2000	Malawi reaches the decision point under the enhanced HIPC initiative
January 2001	Official launch of PRSP process
January 2001	Launch of Thematic Working Groups (TWGs) at the Malawi Institute of Management. Clarification of roles and discussion of terms of reference (ToR)
February 2001	District consultations in all 27 districts, facilitated by the Technical Committee and some TWG members
April 2001	Circulation of first PRSP draft
May 2001	Workshops for comments on first draft by Technical Committee, experts, civil society and TWGs, and charting of the way forward
May 2001	Stakeholders' meeting on draft PRSP document
July 2001	Sharing of TWG costing experience and addressing problems
August 2001	Status reports by TWGs and charting the way forward
September 2001	Media campaign
October 2001	Workshop for comments on first draft by non-government partners
October 2001	Comments on first draft by members of parliament
Nov–Dec 2001	Finalisation of third draft by drafting team
December 2001	Discussion of third draft by principal secretaries
January 2002	Discussion of written submissions/comments by donors
March 2002	Cabinet discussion of PRSP document
March 2002	Submission of final civil society comments, co-ordinated by the Malawi Economic Justice Network (MEJN)
April 2002	Final draft completed, printed and circulated
April 2002	National launch of PRSP document

Source: Malawi Government (2002), Table A1.1

and the budget itself must be fully implemented. Although attempts were made to develop a MTEF approach to budgeting – starting with a few ministries in 1996/97 – it has never been an operational mechanism, with the figures beyond the year of the budget having little or no significance. However, at the outset of the PRSP, attempts were made to restructure expenditure, both between and within sectors, so that sufficient resources were directed towards higher priority sectors/activities, while cutting back on those of lower priority or dropping them altogether. Ministries were also required to improve their financial accountability and transparency. While some attempts have been made to integrate the PRSP into the budget system, particularly at central government level, and the budget system incorporates pro-poor expenditures that relate to funding commitments in the PRSP, it has been observed that sectoral budgets are not funded according to the PRSP and that budgets still focus on inputs rather than relating to outputs. At local government level, the situation is worse with people being ignorant of PRSP indicators and programmes needed to achieve PRSP outputs (Chirwa, 2005). Each of the two major reviews of the MTEF carried out during the 1999/2000 and 2000/2001 fiscal years concluded that the framework had failed to meet its objectives. Financial accountability and transparency were found to be inadequate. Ministries had only partly practised activity-based or programme budgeting and line-budgeting had been reasserted. In terms of its potential impact on PRSP implementation, the most important shortcoming was that patterns of actual expenditure often bore little resemblance to the budget itself. Expenditure ceilings were regularly violated by line ministries and other government agencies. In addition, ministries continued to allocate the largest amount of resources to personal emoluments and non-essential items of expenditure, leaving materials and transport underfunded. Effectively, it is now generally accepted that the MTEF was never operational and more recently the government has concentrated its efforts on annual expenditure management and control.

Progress in implementing the MPRSP: Annual Progress Reports

Implementation of a PRSP entails ensuring that actual public sector expenditure, both government and donor funded, is consistent with PRSP allocations, and that the policies described in the PRSP are carried out. Implementation of the Malawi PRSP started in 2002 and ended in 2005. The first progress report covering the 2002/2003 fiscal year concluded that the implementation of the MPRSP had been unsatisfactory as actual funds allocated for pro-poor activities had been substantially lower than those envisaged in the strategy paper (see table 4.3). One of the main reasons for this was that Malawi's economic programme supported by the IMF's Poverty Reduction and Growth Facility (PRGF) had been off track since November 2001. This led to suspension of external budgetary assistance and to increased recourse to domestic borrowing to cover large budget deficits. As a result, the stock of domestic debt increased from 26.017 billon Malawi kwachas (MK) at the end of June 2002 to MK741 billion at the end of June 2004, before falling slightly to MK564 billon by the end of June 2005. The debt service needs of this domestic debt required more resources, so the resources available for financing pro-poor activities were reduced. The data in table 4.3 also show that some pro-poor activities were not even allocated resources, whereas non-priority activities received more resources than were envisaged in the MPRSP. The first progress report did not analyse in detail the implementation of the sectoral and policy reforms identified in the MPRSP.

Table 4.3: Comparison of shares of the allocation of resources by pillar

Activity	2002/2003 MPRSP	2002/2003 budget	2003/2004 MPRSP	2003/2004 budget	2004/2005 MPRSP	2004/2005 budget
Total budget	100.0	100.0	100.0	100.0	100.0	100.0
Total MPRSP*	70.1	61.1	74.3	50.2	78.6	60.0
Pillar 1	19.4	15.5	21.4	12.9	26.6	27.8
Pillar 2	33.5	34.4	34.9	25.6	34.2	24.7
Pillar 3	2.9	4.4	4.1	7.0	4.6	3.7
Pillar 4	9.8	6.8	8.6	4.8	7.9	3.8
Cross-cutting	4.0	0.0	4.6	0.0	4.9	0.0
Monitoring & evaluation	0.5	0.0	0.6	0.0	0.5	0.0
Statutory	24.2	32.5	20.5	24.9	16.9	25.4
Statehood	5.7	6.3	5.2	24.9	4.4	14.6

Source: Botolo, B, 'Assessment of Poverty Reduction Strategy in Africa: The Case of Malawi'.
* Totals may not add due to rounding.

Many of these reforms were initiated, but the pace was slower than envisaged in the MPRSP. Examples of this include land policy and privatisation. Nonetheless, substantial progress was reported in tracking pro-poor expenditures, preparing and approving the micro-finance policy, developing the wage policy and developing and passing the new Public Finance Management, Public Audit and Public Procurement Bills.

The second annual progress report concluded that implementation of the MPRSP during the 2003/2004 fiscal year was characterised by policy slippages, particularly in the field of fiscal management, and underfunding of pro-poor activities as compared to the MPRSP. It noted that fiscal indiscipline led to increases in domestic debt, interest rates and inflation. This strained relations with donors, resulting in reduced budgetary assistance. Consequently, the share of resources allocated to pro-poor activities was much lower than planned in the MPRSP. The new government, which took office in May 2004, successfully adopted measures to restore fiscal discipline. An inherent problem with pro-poor expenditures (PPEs) was that since they were supposedly protected and hence could not suffer a cut in budgetary resources, ministries and cost centres prioritised too many activities (including those that were not relevant) as being pro-poor. Hence, there was misallocation of resources. On top of that, ministries are known to have been diverting funds from the identified pro-poor activities. At the same time, resources were sometimes left unused, because cost centres did not know or were not sure how HIPC funds should be utilised. The third annual progress report for the 2004/2005 fiscal year noted that expenditure on protected pro-poor activities had been less than budgeted, except under Pillar 1 (sustainable pro-poor growth).

Experience with MPRSP outcomes

It is probably too early to make a proper assessment of the success or failure of the Malawi PRSP in terms of final results. For this reason, this part of the report focuses on the process and intermediate outcomes. In this regard, what are some of the achievements to date? Civil society groups have expressed the view that the MPRS process has stimulated debate in the country on poverty issues and increased interaction between civil society on the one hand, and the government and donors, on the other hand. With respect to resource inflows, the expected increase in external financial support did not materialise during the first two years of MPRSP implementation. It was assumed that the pledged sum of about US$191.32 million would be received; however, the actual sum received was about US$110.05 million. The shortfall in external financial receipts was in part a consequence of poor macroeconomic management (as noted above), but also further contributed to macroeconomic instability in terms of the unstable exchange rate caused by inadequate supply of foreign exchange, and high interest rates caused by excessive borrowing on the money markets by the government to cover budget deficits.

In terms of growth, the MPRSP assumed that the rate of economic growth would average 4.2 per cent during the implementation period, spurred by the agricultural sector. In each of the three years, the rate of economic growth averaged 3.9 per cent per year, below the average requirement of 6 per cent needed to reduce poverty. The 3.9 per cent would have been sufficient if it had originated in smallholder agriculture, in which the majority of Malawi's poor are engaged. Unfortunately, it did not originate there (see table 4.4).

As regards inflation, during the first year of the Malawi PRSP implementation the outturn was lower than the MPRSP target (see table 4.5). This was made possible by the introduction of strict government expenditure control measures. The following year saw the actual inflation rate exceed the MPRSP target because of laxity in government expenditure control. In the final year of MPRSP implementation, the actual rate of inflation again exceeded the target. This was so not because of weaknesses in expenditure control, but because of drought-related food shortages. With respect to fiscal operations, actual total government revenue as a percentage of GDP exceeded the target every year, except

Table 4.4: Real gross domestic product percentage growth rates by sector (2000-2005)

Sector	2000	2001	2002	2003	2004	2005
Agriculture	5.3	-6.0	2.7	5.9	2.7	-6.7
Small-scale	1.6	-4.8	-0.4	12.4	-1.4	-7.4
Large-scale	21.0	-10.3	14.2	-15.4	20.5	-4.2
Mining and quarrying	10.8	7.5	-38.7	18.6	-11.6	40.1
Manufacturing	-3.0	-14.2	-0.1	3.2	6.9	3.6
Electricity and water	10.2	-7.0	5.8	2.4	7.5	5.8
Construction	-2.2	-4.7	14.1	13.3	10.9	17.1
Distribution	-0.3	1.1	1.6	-0.8	6.9	10.0
Transport and communications	-4.2	-0.6	17.5	8.3	7.2	7.7
Financial and professional services	2.0	-3.0	6.7	6.1	7.3	9.7
Ownership of dwellings	2.6	2.8	2.8	2.8	2.8	2.8
Private, social and community services	2.7	2.9	2.9	2.9	2.9	2.8
Producers of government services	-9.9	0.8	-0.5	1.7	2.3	2.4
Unallocable finance charges	2.4	-0.3	13.5	9.6	7.5	10.0
Real GDP growth at factor cost	0.8	-4.1	2.1	3.9	4.6	2.1

Source: Malawi Economic Report 2005

Table 4.5 Planned macroeconomic targets against outcomes

Target	2002/2003 MPRSP	2002/2003 Outturn	2003/2004 MPRSP	2003/2004 Outturn	2004/2005 MPRSP	2004/2005 Outturn
Real GDP growth rate	3.0	2.9	4.5	4.5	5.2	4.4
Inflation rate	11.5	9.6	5.0	11.6	4.4	15.7
TRG/GDP	26.59	25.87	23.58	34.96	25.16	38.01
TGE/GDP	26.46	33.03	23.36	47.87	25.34	41.54
Deficit/GDP	0.13	−7.15	0.22	−12.92	−0.18	−3.53

N.B. TRG = total government revenue; TRE = total government expenditure; and GDP = gross domestic product
Sources: MPRSP and Economic Report 2005

during the first year of MPRSP implementation. In contrast, actual total government expenditure as percentage of GDP exceeded the target during the entire period of MPRSP implementation. In determining the overall fiscal balance, the MPRSP assumed a surplus in each of the first two years. It was hoped that the surplus would have a positive impact on the economy. As it turned out, deficits were incurred. The third year was less ambitious, but the deficit turned out to be larger than the MPRSP target. In terms of the ultimate objective of poverty reduction, the evidence is that the incidence of poverty hardly changed. Bearing in mind that the measurement of poverty is subjective and subject to statistical errors, the results of the 1998 and 2005 Integrated Household Surveys indicate that the proportion of the population living below the national poverty line fell slightly from 53.9 per cent to 52.4 per cent. There was also a significant increase in the incidence of poverty in urban areas. In rural areas, there was a slight decline in the Central and Southern Regions, but an increase in the Northern Region. The draft comprehensive review of the MPRS noted that the degree of implementation varied across sectors, with many sectors attaining average or below average implementation. In agriculture, food security had not been achieved, but there was an improvement in livestock production. There was also an improvement in most of the non-income (for example, education, health, water and sanitation) measures of poverty over the three years 2002 to 2005.

Malawi Economic Growth Strategy and Malawi Growth and Development Strategy

The Malawi Economic Growth Strategy (MEGS) was formulated from 2002, and was completed and finally launched in 2004. MEGS aimed to complement the MPRS by stimulating private-sector growth and ensuring that the poor are key participants and beneficiaries of economic growth. It owed its origin to a number of missing links in the MPRSP, about which both the government and the private sector were concerned. The first is that the strategies and actions in the MPRSP were insufficient to achieve sustained annual economic growth of at least 6 per cent and thus contribute to poverty reduction. The second is that the 2002/2003 MPRSP review revealed that housing and land policies, among others, were not adequately articulated to effectively contribute to broad-based economic growth. The MPRSP contained a pro-poor growth strategy for stimulating economic growth in ways that directly attack poverty, but it did not articulate the role of the private sector sufficiently. Its focus was on the role of micro- and small-scale enterprises. At the same time, while the MPRSP identified certain sectors in terms of their growth potential, it did not emphasise eliminating obstacles to economy-wide growth. Part I of MEGS sets out the background to the strategy, the framework for delivering growth and the strategy for dealing with the macroeconomic constraints that affect enterprises. Part II analyses the main sectors of the economy, and the strategies for the growth of the core and other sub-sectors of the economy. There is also a review of key public institutions that support and regulate the private sector.

The process of developing MEGS was less consultative than the one employed to develop the MPRSP. Because a broad spectrum of stakeholders were consulted during the preparation of the latter, it was not considered necessary to go through a new round of consultations, which, in any case, was considered to be resource intensive and expensive. The Director-General of the then Department of Economic Planning and Development (DEPD) co-ordinated the development of the MEGS. A taskforce, comprising personnel from key economic ministries and institutions and supported by a team from the DEPD and the National Action Group Secretariat, was established. There was a series of consultations with the private sector and other key public-sector organisations. Thereafter, the document was considered by the National Acton Group, which comprises key economic ministers, heads of donor organisations and leaders of the private sector. Finally, the document was submitted to the cabinet for approval before implementation.

At the time of writing this case study (August 2006), the government was in the process of replacing the MPRSP and MEGS with a new strategy called the Malawi Growth and Development Strategy (MGDS), which was being prepared under similar institutional arrangements. MGDS draws upon and combines critical issues in the Vision 2020, the Millennium Development Goals (MDGs) and other development strategies and is consistent with the vision of President Bingu wa Mutharika. Like the MEGS, the MGDS focuses on achieving strong sustainable economic growth that will enable Malawians to create their own wealth through economic empowerment. The strategy is comprehensive, with five pillars (the original four pillars in the MPRSP and infrastructure, emphasis on which is highly desirable). Improving food security, so as to ensure that Malawi is a hunger-free nation, features prominently. Attempts have been made to incorporate the cross-cutting issues of HIV/AIDS, gender, environment and science and technology into the five pillars. Key stakeholders, principally the private sector, civil society and donors, have been consulted. However, the drafts of the MGDS were found to suffer from some of the weaknesses that we identified with the MPRS, including insufficient selectivity and prioritisation. We hope that some of these issues will be addressed as the MGDS is further developed and implemented, as discussed below. Given the capacity constraints in government, absence of a functioning medium-term expenditure framework (MTEF), the vulnerability of the Malawi economy to exogenous shocks and uncertainties about future aid flows, we also believe it will be important to see the MGDS as a broad statement, with a good deal of flexibility about implementation, and not as a multi-year financial or expenditure plan.

III Quality of the strategy and its implementation

This section seeks to answer a set of questions about the nature and quality of the Poverty Reduction Strategy process in Malawi. It focuses on the whole process - including the PRS documents, the process of drawing them up and strategy implementation, including the link with budget and other government processes - not just on the strategy documents themselves. The section also looks at the original MPRSP, and the ways it was implemented and evolved over time, and also at the new Malawi Growth and Development Strategy (published in draft form at the time of writing) that will guide policy over the years ahead.

Ownership

Ownership is a complex issue. There is ownership by officials in the central economic ministries; ownership at the highest political level, by cabinet and the president; ownership by officials and ministers in the key implementing ministries; ownership by those responsible for implementation at the local and district level; national ownership as endorsed by national democratic processes through parliament; ownership by other stakeholders, including the private sector and civil society; and ownership - or at least a degree of understanding of the strategy - among the general population. In different ways all these forms of ownership are likely to be relevant to success or failure in implementing a national strategy. Both comments made to us during our research and experience with implementation over the three years 2002-2005 suggest that for most of these dimensions, there was relatively weak country ownership of the original MPRS, adopted in 2002. It was widely seen, both within government, (other than in the core ministries that led design of the strategy) and outside it, more as a process undertaken to meet donor and BWI requirements for HIPC debt relief than as a development strategy deriving from domestic processes. This is also evident from the record in implementation. Some priority was given in successive budgets to protecting social expenditures, as the strategy required, although this appears to have been seen more as something donors required, less as a national priority. Critically, however, the lack of ownership at a political level was demonstrated by decisions to depart significantly from priorities set out in annual budgets. It has been suggested that the figures given in table 4.3 may overstate the extent of departure from MPRS objectives, but even so it is clear that the departure was substantial. Donors initially accepted the MPRS as a basis for their support, but then suspended support as it became clear it was not being implemented - illustrating the problems of adopting a strategy as a framework for donor support when there is insufficient national ownership.

Certainly there was a degree of ownership by the small number of officials in central departments who drew up the original strategy. The team responsible - the MPRS Technical Committee and the National Steering Committee of principal secretaries to which it reported - did a good job in preparing what appeared to be a coherent strategy, which was approved by cabinet. Although sector and implementing ministries made considerable contributions to the process through the Technical Working Groups, final decisions on content of the strategy were made by the core drafting team, subject to approval by the Technical and Steering Committees. For this and other reasons, it appears that outside the core team even the key sector and implementing ministries did not, initially at least, feel wholly part of the process, although they appear to have become more engaged over the years of implementation. At the time of writing, only very few ministries – possibly only the Ministry of Health – had fully aligned their strategies with the MPRS (and since the health strategy predated the MPRS, it is more accurate to say that the MPRS incorporated the ministry strategy). Moreover, understanding about what the strategy seeks to achieve appears to be extremely limited where in some ways it matters most – at the district level, which is responsible for so much of the implementation. This is partly due to the very limited outreach carried out by central government.

Outside of government, no formal parliamentary approval is required, although members of parliament were involved in discussions leading to up to the MPRS, and there was a parliamentary workshop in October 2001. Somewhat paradoxically, it seems that the group with the strongest sense of ownership of the MPRS may have been civil society. The consultation process in drawing up the MPRS was extensive, and while, as noted in section II, there were some weaknesses and the relatively well-organised civil society organisation (CSO) movement in Malawi feels that its inputs were not fully reflected in the final document, evidence suggests that that civil society feels a stronger sense of ownership than any other group. Certainly, CSOs have put and are putting much effort into spreading knowledge of the MPRS among groups responsible for its implementation – among parliamentarians and elsewhere – and told us that they stand ready to do the same kind of outreach for the new MGDS. That said, there are questions about how representative many CSOs really are: with the exception of faith-based organisations, few CSOs in Malawi have a solid grass roots foundation or strong membership base. They also differ in structure, with some being single-issue NGOs and some addressing a broader spectrum of concerns, and are often funded from external sources.

The private sector, on the other hand, felt the original MPRS paid too little attention to the needs of business. The government sought to right the imbalance with the adoption in 2004 of the MEGS, and its subsequent incorporation into the MGDS.

For the future, the MGDS seems to offer the prospect of wider and more genuine country ownership. The government sees it as home grown, and fitting with the vision of the President (who previously had responsibility for the MEGS, when he was Minister of Economic Planning and Development) to develop the country's productive and export capacity, achieving sustainable economic growth through empowering people, and to provide the infrastructure and operating environment needed for a successful private sector. Most donors have deliberately stood back, giving the government space in which to develop its own strategy. The MGDS has drawn on separate consultations on the MEGS and on the government review of the MPRSP, as well as on three major regional consultation meetings, including those with members of parliament carried out in parallel with a process of costing and prioritising the MGDS. Therefore, while consultation was less extensive than with the original MPRS, our fieldwork discussions suggest that most domestic stakeholders – CSOs as well as businesses – feel adequately engaged with the process. The MGDS was to extend for a period of five years, beyond the date of the next election. We believe therefore that it will be helpful to do more to develop national forms of accountability, in particular to parliament, to make it completely clear that the government is accountable for the strategy and its implementation to the people of Malawi, not to development partners; and that the strategy is to some degree at least a truly nationally owned – not just government-owned – strategy. We hope it will be possible to find a way to present the MGDS formally to parliament, and to stimulate genuine parliamentary discussion and debate.

Nature and quality of the MPRS

As noted in section II, the MPRS was based on four strategic 'pillars': sustainable pro-poor growth; human capital development; improving the quality of life for the most vulnerable; and good governance, together with a number of key cross-cutting issues such as HIV/AIDS and gender. While the strategy itself is generally seen as coherent and comprehensive – and was certainly judged adequate for support by the international financial institutions (IFIs) and other donors – it is now widely accepted that there were some important weaknesses.

First, there was insufficient selectivity and prioritisation. While a national development strategy should be comprehensive, in a country like Malawi, which has limited capacity, it is essential to clearly identify priorities for action. This also appears to be a weakness in the drafts of the Malawi Growth and Development Strategy that we saw, a weakness we hope will be addressed as the strategy is finalised and implemented. For example, if improving food security is a top priority for the immediate future, then the strategy should say so and say what is to be done to achieve it, such as improving water harvesting and encouraging commercial farming. We also think the strategy should identify priority policy changes, some of which may have few expenditure implications, as well as expenditure priorities. While it is right to try to cost the first year of implementation, and to illustrate the full cost over time of major capital projects, we think it would be a mistake prior to the strategy's finalisation and implementation to attach much weight to any costings developed for future years or to try to draw up anything like a five-year expenditure plan. The uncertainties, both about what will be feasible and about future aid flows, are too great. It would be more sensible to think in terms – as we believe was planned – of various possible scenarios for future levels of expenditure, exploring what might be achieved under different scenarios, with final decisions made within the strategic guidelines in annual budgets.

The second weakness was that there was little if any consideration of alternative strategies. While the Malawi Poverty Reduction Strategy covered a wide range of issues, most of the policies set out were those already tried (with limited success) under previous structural adjustment programmes – including, for example, policies such as the focus on improving the efficiency of the financial system as a way to reduce interest rates (when high government borrowing was the real problem).

The strategy's growth/private sector/infrastructure pillar was generally seen to be weak, and the private sector felt the MPRS did not sufficiently address its concerns. Consideration of the sources of growth was narrowly focused on macroeconomic stabilisation, access to credit and rural infrastructure. There was little attention to other key factors, such as improving the management of statutory and parastatal organisations; issues of human and natural resources; the internal and external economic environment; trade policy issues; and relevant cultural, social and political factors. Following consultations between the Department of Economic Planning and Development and the private sector, in 2004 the Government of Malawi adopted the MEGS, designed to complement the MPRS. At the time of writing, this was being fully integrated into the new MGDS. Again, we hope the MGDS will identify the immediate priorities – for example, strengthening particular road or rail links; reducing interest rates; reducing taxes on businesses or making them more predictable; improving the reliability of water supplies in urban areas; improving the reliability of the electricity supply; and developing the entire financial sector to improve access to credit. As noted elsewhere, some of the relevant policy changes will have few if any implications for government spending: that does not reduce their importance, but may make them easier to implement.

While the strategy identifies a number of cross-cutting issues, only HIV/AIDS was beginning to be mainstreamed into sector policies at the time of writing. Many see the analysis of gender issues as seriously inadequate, with little attempt to mainstream gender into MPRS policies.

The Malawi Poverty Reduction Strategy targets fell short of meeting the Millennium Development Goals, and there was no attempt in the MPRS to assess how much extra assistance Malawi could effectively absorb to make faster progress towards meeting the MDGs. Nor did the draft MGDS contain such an assessment, although we understood that the government intended to carry one out during the first year of the MGDS. In addition, we understood that the final version of the MGDS was to contain two scenarios, with one of the two demonstrating the faster progress that could be made if more resources were available. Given the possibility of a significant increase in donor flows to Malawi to accelerate progress to the MDGs, these seemed to be useful exercises to carry out.

Although there were monitoring indicators in the MPRSP and the subsequent Monitoring and Evaluation Master Plan, the government did not create an effective monitoring and evaluation system, a weakness that the MGDS intends to address. We welcome the action to strengthen relevant monitoring and data systems, including at the district level and at the National Statistical Office, and the results framework built into the MGDS, which can be used to develop a monitoring system linked to actions.

Finally, we found that the government could have usefully put more effort into outreach to communicate the strategy once it was adopted, explaining it both to the general population and to those on the ground responsible for its implementation. The strategy is more likely to be sustainable and to be implemented, if it is seen and accepted as a national as well as a government strategy. This would involve activities such as running workshops for district officials, and producing a widely available summary of the document, translated into local languages. These activities have all been undertaken in respect of the MPRS by civil society organisations such as the Malawi Economic Justice Network, and this is very welcome. However, with the launch of the new MGDS, we hope the task will also be seen as a government responsibility. For a number of reasons, not least because the period of the strategy extends beyond the next elections, we found it to be important to make the effort to establish a broad national consensus that the strategy is the right road map for Malawi. This is particularly important to ensure that the strategy is understood by those responsible for implementing it at the local level and that it is incorporated into district development plans.

How well has the strategy been implemented?

However good or well written a strategy is, it is worthless if not implemented. One development partner to whom we spoke said we should ask the question: had the Malawi Poverty Reduction Strategy made any difference to anything in practice? His clear implication was that it had not. Our judgement is that up to 2004 at least, the MPRS may have had some minor impact on budget allocations and outturns – but probably not much.

As noted in section II, it was intended that the MPRS would be implemented in annual budgets, using a medium-term expenditure framework (MTEF) as a bridge between the multi-year MPRS and annual budgets. Attempts were made to encourage sector ministries to identify 'pro-poor' expenditures, with the intention that these expenditures would be protected in the event of budget difficulties – and sector ministries maintain that the so-called 'protected pro-poor expenditures' (PPEs) were indeed protected to an extent. However, we doubt whether this is an accurate measure of MPRS implementation, given the incentives for sector ministries to classify as wide as possible a range of their expenditures as PPEs.

In addition, as also discussed in section II and elsewhere, budget outturns over the period bore little relation to budget plans – and the substantial overspends were not on MPRS priorities. As already noted, the MTEF never operated effectively (the draft MGDS implies it will be resuscitated). Following persistent inability to control public expenditure, Malawi went off-track with its Poverty Reduction and Growth Facility (PRGF) in November 2001. Donor budget support (which represented 23 per cent of budgeted revenue in 2001/02) was suspended. However, the Government of Malawi continued spending and financed the deficit through domestic borrowing. As a result, the domestic debt/GDP ratio jumped from 8 per cent in June 2001 to 25 per cent in June 2004. Real interest rates also jumped, leading to a massive increase in domestic interest payments as a proportion of government spending and GDP. Instead of the increased share of expenditure promised in the PRSP, pro-poor expenditure was crowded out by the growing interest bill.

Some of this failure in the link between the MPRS and annual budgets could be attributed to weak financial management capacity. There is no doubt that financial management capacity needs strengthening. The government has been working for many years on an 'integrated financial management information system' (IFMIS), and only recently decided in effect to cut losses on past work and implement a system developed and used in Tanzania. Stronger financial management capacity is also needed in implementing ministries, to ensure that spending priorities really do reflect national priorities as set out in the strategy; and to ensure that these spending priorities are carried through effectively at the local level. However, we found that the finance ministry had managed to deliver expenditures within and in line with the budget in the year leading up to the present study – so weak financial systems can only be a partial explanation of the record of poor MPRS implementation.

We also note the emphasis in the draft Malawi Growth and Development Strategy on the need for all departmental and sector expenditure plans and budget bids to be consistent with the MGDS. We believe the MGDS should become the central feature of the annual budget system, as this emphasis implies, and suggest a number of steps that will help make this an operational reality.

First, such an operational reality requires development of an effective challenge function in the Ministry of Finance budget division: departments' priorities and annual budget bids need to be justified in terms of the MGDS and the Ministry of Finance should ensure that they are. Sending circulars to departments asking them to prepare budget submissions taking account of the MGDS is unlikely by itself to secure the desired outcome. For the immediate future, we suggest that a relatively simple approach of Ministry of Finance scrutiny and challenge of departmental bids may be the best way to try to ensure the MGDS is implemented. We doubt whether the concept of MGDS-related expenditures is useful: in principle the entire budget should derive, directly or indirectly, from the expression of national priorities set out in the MGDS. We also doubt whether reviving the pro-poor expenditures mechanism will be helpful. At the same time, while implementing a functioning MTEF may be a useful long-term ambition, we doubt whether it is realistic or sensible to devote scarce resources to it in the short term.

Second, making the MGDS central to the budget process will require a close working relationship between the Ministry of Economic Planning and Development (MEPD), as guardian of the strategy, and Ministry of Finance budget division. In this context, it was suggested to us that it would be helpful to merge the two departments. In our view, however, that would neither guarantee the level of co-operation needed, nor be necessary to achieve it. With or without a merger of the two departments, MEPD staff should join with Ministry of Finance staff in challenging departments' budget bids and seeking to ensure consistency with the MGDS.

There are also aspects of the MPRS – and now the MGDS – that require actions by the government, but which do not necessarily have budgetary consequences: for example, simplifying regulations affecting businesses; reforming the tax system; implementing investment incentives in a predictable non-discriminatory manner; or reducing delays in processing of land applications. Again, our impression is that progress has been slow, possibly reflecting the problems of passing legislation through parliament during a period of intense domestic political activity, other than legislation such as the Public Financial Management, Public Audit and Procurement Acts, which could be presented to parliament and passed into law as part of the annual budget process. In future, we hope that the Ministry of Finance and Ministry of Economic Planning and Development together can work to ensure that where such policy commitments are made in the MGDS, they are carried through and executed effectively.

Last and perhaps the most important of all, is the question of what practical impact the MPRS has had in achieving results on the ground. At the time of writing, the government had carried out two annual progress reports and was engaged in its own comprehensive review of achievements over the whole MPRS period. We saw an early draft of this review and hope that when completed it will throw further light on the issue. However, we found that while a Monitoring and Evaluation Committee was established in 2002, when the MPRS was launched, it only developed and launched a monitoring and evaluation master plan in November 2004. In general, capacity for gathering data about progress in poverty reduction and growth, through the National Statistical Office, remains weak. It is encouraging that the MGDS clearly recognises the need for a plan for better measurement of outcomes and results – and it will be important to implement this. We also welcome the intention to follow the example of some other countries and establish an arrangement for periodic independent monitoring and evaluation of implementation of the MGDS and support given to it by development partners.

IV Quality of support given by external partners

This section assesses the support being given to Malawi by development partners – both multilateral organisations and bilateral partners. Have they given appropriate support to the PRS process, while leaving the government the space it needs to set national priorities? Have partners acted to align their support behind the priorities set out in the MPRS? Are they moving to improve the effectiveness of their support, reducing administrative demands on government and implementing global agreements to harmonise donor procedures and practices?

Support for preparation and review of the MPRS

In general, external support for the process of drawing up and reviewing progress in the Malawi Poverty Reduction Strategy was appropriate: external partners gave the government space to design its own strategy and did not seek to lead the process. External funding financed the extensive consultation process on the MPRSP. IMF/World Bank Joint Staff Assessments (JSAs) and Joint Staff Advisory Notes (JSANs) on the MPRSP and MPRS annual progress reports were helpful and to the point. More recently, external partners have gone to even greater lengths in relation to the Malawi Growth and Development Strategy than they did with the original MPRSP to leave space for the government to make its own decisions and set its own priorities, limiting their involvement in the process to providing valuable technical support only. One donor we spoke to felt unhappy about lack of involvement in the process and would have liked more dialogue earlier, but most felt that by standing back they were helping to achieve an end result more fully owned by the government. In parallel, there has been strong and continuing donor support for the preparation and implementation of the one operational sector strategy – the health sector sector-wide approach (SWAp) – and we hope this support will be extended to other sector strategies when they are developed.

Nevertheless, as noted above, there was a widely held view that the original MPRS was adopted only as a condition for HIPC debt relief, and indeed its priorities reflected quite closely what were thought to be donor priorities at the time, with an emphasis on poverty-reducing expenditures, and less emphasis on fostering the conditions for private-sector led growth. This suggests that continued efforts will be needed by all stakeholders to ensure that the new MGDS really is – and is seen to be – a nationally owned and developed strategy. This requires restraint from all development partners, who need to recognise the importance of developing country-owned policies that will be implemented in a sustained manner over the years ahead, not abandoned once debt relief is secured.

Alignment of support from development partners

Has support from the IFIs and other partners been grounded, as intended, in the Malawi Poverty Reduction Strategy or have external partners sought to impose different, separate conditions? Alternatively, have donor partners financed projects not included as priorities?

Most donors have been willing – or at least say they have been willing – to use the MPRS as the framework for their support. The IMF said its PRGF was fully in line with the MPRS, and at the time of writing expected it to similarly be in line with the new MGDS. The 2003 UK Country Assistance Plan explicitly supports MPRSP objectives; the 2004 World Bank Country Assistance Strategy is aligned behind the MPRSP pillars; EC assistance is similarly aligned with the MPRSP as set out in its 2001 seven country strategy paper. Four donors (the UK, EC, Sweden and Norway) provide budget support and have established the Common Approach to Budget Support (CABS) group to interface with government, and there are prospects for the proportion of aid channelled in this way to increase, and for new partners to join the group. We found that the World Bank, UK, EC, Canada and Norway all said they would align their strategies with the MGDS, with most changing their scheduling to facilitate this and an initial attempt to identify gaps in support and to make an inventory of donor analytical work. At the sector level, a wider group of partners has come together to support the health sector SWAp; and the government is planning to develop similar SWAps in other sectors, including in agriculture and education. We are, nevertheless, concerned that some of the conditions set for reaching the HIPC completion point appear to relate to policy details that do not appear essential to the overall strategy, and which may not in all cases reflect the government's priorities.

That said, for much of the MPRS period failures in macroeconomic management led to a suspension of IMF support, which in effect led to both a breakdown in MPRS implementation and the withholding of donor support. Moreover, all donors still give support in project form, some in effect to finance public-sector activities, some to support facilities and services provided by NGOs. Meanwhile, some donors remain resistant to providing sector support, still less budget support. The Ministry of Finance and sector ministries say they are not always aware of donor-funded activities, although they are trying to collect better information, especially in sectors where there are SWAps. Clearly, even if the macroeconomic situation had been better, it would have been – and remains – difficult for the government to plan to implement its development strategy effectively without such information, which is needed both to inform budget priority setting (if a donor is already building a health centre in an area, then there is no need for one funded from the budget) and for future financial and resource planning (new facilities funded by donors usually need staffing and upkeep). The MGDS and annual budgets should in principle cover all relevant expenditures, whether financed from taxation, borrowing or donor resources. In future it will be important for the government to capture all relevant donor expenditure and planned expenditure, whether it is provided through the budget or in project support. In principle this should be easier to achieve now that the bank accounts of donor projects have been centralised in the Reserve Bank.

Over much of the period under consideration here, donors withheld funds because of governance and other implementation failures, and appeared less willing to switch to budget or sector support than in other countries. Where they do provide such support, they appear less willing than elsewhere to enter into long-term multi-year commitments. However, with the better implementation experience over the year leading up to the research, and with the launch of the Malawi Growth and Development Strategy, we saw an opportunity that external partners and the government together could take to achieve a step change in alignment of support. This would involve three key elements: a substantially increased level of budget support; priority to the development of sector SWAps; and a major effort to integrate and link the MGDS with annual budgets.

Learning from Experience

First then would be a substantially increased level of budget support, building on CABS, made more predictable by donors turning the commitments they already make for the year ahead into firm multi-year commitments. The government should recognise that encouraging donors to switch substantially to budget support will take a lengthy period of confidence building. And donors should recognise that for the arrangement to work, they should agree on a single, and limited, policy assessment framework (PAF) drawn from the comprehensive matrix set out in the MGDS. It will, however, take time to build sufficient confidence that the Ministry of Finance will maintain financial control and enforce the link between the MGDS, annual budgets and departmental expenditures.

For this reason it may be sensible over the next few years to also give priority to the development of sector SWAps, building on the experience in the health sector. The Ministry of Finance prefers budget support to SWAps – as do we – as being less likely to undermine national priority setting and budget discipline. However, we see sector-wide support as preferable to individual projects, unless these are fully incorporated and monitored as part of national or sector plans. Moreover, over the next few years we see a number of additional advantages in developing SWAps: they should help strengthen departments' human resources and sector management capacities; they may help provide greater stability in sector policies, which in the past have often been subject to change whenever ministers or senior officials change or there is a change in donor preferences; they should help maintain consistency between sector policies and the MGDS; and they should help keep donors focused on medium-term priorities and reduce the tendency of some donors to give priority to high-visibility projects with short-term payoffs. At the same time, in other countries, donor groupings supporting SWAps have proved an effective mechanism for disciplining 'rogue' donors – providing a form of insurance against sudden shifts in behaviour by individual donors.

These developments need to be underpinned by a major effort, as discussed above, to integrate and link the MGDS with annual budgets, developing financial management and information capacity as needed, in the Ministry of Finance, the MEPD and in sector ministries. Building donor confidence will require these links to be explicit and highly transparent: sector plans and budgets should flow and be seen to flow from the MGDS. We commend the idea that was under discussion at the time of our research of a donor-funded SWAp to support strengthening public financial management.

These changes would facilitate one further feature that we believe to be of continuing importance for Malawi: the availability of emergency finance when the country faces unexpected adverse shocks. We note that it proved possible to arrange extra concessional finance from donors and IFIs over the year leading up to the case study highlighted here to meet the food emergency of that period, but think that implementing changes as suggested above would make such assistance easier to arrange if needed in future.

Could a significant increase in donor financing for the MDGs be used effectively?

There is now at least the possibility of a substantial increase in aid flows to Malawi. The policy environment is better than it has been for many years and there is a prospect of 100 per cent debt reduction. Malawi has been selected for the US Threshold Program to help work towards eligibility for Millennium Challenge Corporation (MCC) finance.

Meanwhile, other traditional donors to Malawi are aiming to increase their future funding to the country as in other sub-Saharan African countries. We believe that a new country-owned MGDS and other improvements in the process – especially improved financial management at all levels and improved modalities for support by development partners – should significantly increase Malawi's capacity to absorb aid effectively. As a result, Malawi should be able to make better use of aid flows already available, as well as to make effective use of steadily increasing aid flows over the years ahead.

We would therefore encourage the Government of Malawi, as we believe was planned at the time of writing, to make an assessment of how much aid could usefully be absorbed and help towards meeting the Millennium Development Goals, if it were available. Such a scenario would be a useful assessment to have in future discussions with development partners. Moreover, a Malawi Growth and Development Strategy illustrating different possible scenarios would be consistent with the suggestion that the strategy should focus on short-term priorities and medium- and longer-term possibilities, to be translated each year into annual budgets, rather than seeking to construct a five-year expenditure plan.

Donor co-ordination and harmonisation of practices and procedures

In Malawi, relatively little progress has been made so far in implementing the global agreements to better harmonise and co-ordinate donor practices and procedures set out in the Paris declaration. The Ministry of Finance, Debt and Aid Management Division is responsible for co-ordination of external assistance, and there are various local donor co-ordination groups, including at the sector level. At the time of writing there had been a recent stock take of necessary actions measured against the Paris Declaration baseline. As noted above, much remains to be done if the government is to have a complete picture of donor activities in Malawi; and it will take further efforts to provide the kind of country leadership needed to make progress in better co-ordinating and harmonising donor practices and procedures.

Without such an effort, there is a risk that as aid flows increase, donors will be placing an ever-increasing burden on government ministers and senior officials, as numbers of parallel reporting requirements, donor missions and local consultation committees expand. Key officials in sector ministries told us that handling donor committees and missions takes between 30 per cent and 50 per cent of their time.

Experience in other countries suggests a number of approaches that could be tried. For example, persuading more partners to channel more of their support through the budget, or at least through sector basket funds, can greatly reduce the burden, particularly where government financial management and auditing systems are strong enough to persuade donors to dispense with parallel reporting requirements. The burden of interacting with local donor groups can also be reduced by establishing a regular and well-spaced annual cycle of consultation meetings, timed to fit with key decision points in the annual budget cycle; and by encouraging donors to rely on one of their number to provide expertise in each sector or topic, rather than all wishing to be represented at each meeting. The burden of receiving incoming aid missions can be reduced by declaring 'quiet times' of year, when missions are not welcome; and by agreeing targets for reduced numbers of missions and then collecting and publishing data about numbers of missions from different partners (a process of 'naming and shaming'). Finally, the government should be ready on occasion to say 'no' to aid offered in the wrong modalities or in the wrong form.

Experience elsewhere is that this task of 'aid co-ordination' – organising donors – has to be led by the Ministry of Finance, and that in a country like Malawi, where aid accounts for a substantial proportion of the annual budget, extra effort in this respect has a significant pay off. We therefore strongly welcome and encourage the stated intention of the Ministry of Finance to work with development partners to put such arrangements in place in Malawi. At the time of writing, the proposed arrangements were set to include:

- Building capacity in the Ministry of Finance to provide leadership and co-ordination
- Confirming donors' agreement to align their support behind MGDS priorities
- Agreement on a set of good practices by donors and by the government, covering issues ranging from frequency and timing of missions to accounting and reporting policies and practices
- Agreement on monitoring and evaluation arrangements
- An agreed action plan for all parties, with monitorable benchmarks

V   Main findings and recommendations

The Malawi Poverty Reduction Strategy was developed in the early 2000s at the request of the Bretton Woods Institutions, and as in other countries suffered from a widely held perception of being developed simply in order to qualify for HIPC debt relief. It was intended that it should draw on a number of previous national development strategies, though in practice we think the linkage was weak. It was developed with a relatively strong degree of public participation, although there were some weaknesses in the process. After its adoption, the government identified one missing element – a lack of attention to ways to stimulate private sector-led growth – and complemented the MPRS with the Malawi Economic Growth Strategy. However, the main problems that emerged were in implementation. There was at best only a modest connection between the strategy and annual budget allocations, and even less relationship with budget outturns. Because of failures in macroeconomic policy, donor support was less than anticipated, and final results, in terms of growth and measured changes in poverty levels, were disappointing.

We have tried to identify the main causes of failures and successes in MPRS implementation, and to draw out lessons for the future: that is, the lessons for the new Malawi Growth and Development Strategy and its implementation. A number of these conclusions may also have relevance in other countries with similar experiences of mixed success in implementation of their initial poverty reduction strategies.

Successes and failures in the MPRS and its implementation

Ownership: the MPRS in the national context

How far was the strategy nationally 'owned' and how far was it perceived as imposed from outside? Ownership is widely seen as critical to successful implementation, but is a complex issue with many dimensions. Comments made to us in our discussions and experience with implementation over the three years up to the study (2002–2005) suggest that in most dimensions there was relatively weak country ownership of the original MPRS (adopted 2002). Other than in the core ministries that led design of the strategy, it was seen more as a process undertaken to meet donor and BWI requirements than as a development strategy deriving from domestic processes.

Within government, the lack of ownership at a political level was evident from the record in implementation, demonstrated by decisions over most of the period covered by the MPRS that departed significantly from government expenditure priorities. Outside the core team, even the key sector and implementing ministries did not, initially at least, feel wholly part of the process, although they appeared to become more engaged over the years of implementation. At the time of writing, very few ministries – possibly only the Ministry of Health – had fully aligned their strategies with the MPRS. Moreover ownership, or even understanding, of what the strategy sought to achieve appeared to be extremely limited at the district level, which was responsible for so much MPRS implementation.

Outside of government, no formal parliamentary approval was required for the strategy, although MPs were involved in discussions leading to up to it. The private sector felt the original MPRS paid too little attention to the needs of business. As a result, the government sought to right the balance with the adoption in 2004 of the MEGS, and its subsequent incorporation into the MGDS.

Somewhat paradoxically, it seems that the group with the strongest sense of ownership of the MPRS may have been civil society. While CSOs felt that their inputs were not fully reflected in the final document, evidence suggests that they may feel a stronger sense of ownership than any other group. Certainly, CSOs have spread and are spreading knowledge of the MPRS among groups responsible for its implementation.

Nature and quality of the strategy

Was the strategy itself well conceived? It is now widely accepted that there were some important weaknesses:

- There was insufficient selectivity and prioritisation. While a national development strategy should be comprehensive, it is essential clearly to identify priorities for action in a country like Malawi, which has limited capacity.
- There was little if any consideration of alternative strategies. While the MPRS covered a wide range of issues, most of the policies set out were those already tried, with limited success, under previous structural adjustment programmes.
- The strategy's growth/private sector/infrastructure pillar was generally seen to be weak; as noted above, this was subsequently addressed with the adoption in 2004 of the MEGS.
- While the strategy identifies a number of cross-cutting issues, only HIV/AIDS is beginning to be mainstreamed into sector policies. Many see the analysis of gender issues as seriously inadequate, with little attempt to mainstream gender into MPRS policies.
- MPRS targets fell short of meeting the Millennium Development Goals, and there was no attempt in the MPRS to assess how much extra assistance Malawi could effectively absorb to make faster progress towards meeting the MDGs.

- Although there were monitoring indicators in the MPRSP and the subsequent Monitoring and Evaluation Master Plan, the government failed to create an effective monitoring and evaluation system.
- Finally, we believe the government could usefully have put more effort into outreach to communicate the strategy once it was adopted, explaining it both to the general population and to those on the ground responsible for its implementation. The strategy is more likely to be sustainable, and to be implemented, if it is seen and accepted as a national as well as government strategy; and it needs to be understood by those responsible for implementing it at the local level – and, for example, incorporated into district development plans.

The record of implementation

As noted above, the record of implementation is poor. Over most of the MPRS period, budget expenditures showed little relationship to MPRS priorities. While weaknesses in financial management and failure to make the MTEF operational will have contributed, these are only part of the explanation, with lack of ownership and political commitment playing a larger part. For the future it will also be important to develop a more effective challenge function in the Ministry of Finance, to seek to ensure departmental expenditure plans are linked with the strategy.

Progress has also been slow in implementing aspects of the MPRS that require policy actions, but do not have budgetary consequences. Again, core departments need to play a more effective role in ensuring that policy commitments in the strategy are carried through and executed effectively.

The government has been slow to create the monitoring and evaluation capacity needed to ensure that the strategy ultimately produces results. We welcome the progress being made in this respect, and also the intention to establish a mechanism for periodic independent monitoring and evaluation of implementation of the strategy and support being given to it by development partners.

Alignment and volume of support by development partners

In principle, most donors have been willing (or say they have) to align their support with the MPRS, though in practice over most of the MPRS period this was not tested because of the breakdown in macroeconomic management and MPRS implementation, and consequent withdrawal of donor support. At the time of writing there is the prospect, which we welcome, of an increased volume of support coming in the form of budget or sector-wide support. Nonetheless, some donors remain resistant to this trend and most continue to provide support in the form of individual projects.

For the future, it will be important for the government to know of all relevant donor expenditure and planned expenditure, whether it is provided through the budget or in project support, to inform budget priority setting and resource planning. In principle this should be easier to achieve now that the bank accounts of donor projects have been centralised in the Reserve Bank.

While budget support linked to a single policy assessment framework agreed between donors and the government will in the long term be the best modality to ensure donor alignment, we recognise that encouraging donors to switch substantially to budget support in Malawi will take a significant period of confidence building. For this reason it may be sensible over the next few years to give priority to the development of sectoral support through sector SWAps, building on the experience in the health sector. They should help strengthen departments' human resources and sector management capacities, may help provide greater stability in sector policies, and maintain consistency between sector policies and the Malawi Growth and Development Strategy, and they should help keep donors focused on medium-term priorities, and maintain consistency in donor behaviour through peer pressure.

These developments need to be underpinned by a major effort, as discussed above, to link the strategy transparently to annual budgets, developing financial management and information capacity as needed. Building donor confidence will require these links to be explicit and highly transparent.

We believe improvements being made in the strategy and implementation process – especially improved financial management at all levels, and improved modalities for support by development partners – will significantly increase Malawi's capacity to absorb aid effectively. The country should as a result be able to make better use of aid flows already available, as well as to make effective use of steadily increasing aid flows over the years ahead. We therefore encourage the Government of Malawi to make an assessment of how much aid could usefully be absorbed and could help towards meeting the MDGs, if that aid were available (this was thought to be planned at the time of writing).

Donor co-ordination and harmonisation of practices and procedures

Relatively little progress has been made in implementing in Malawi the global agreements to better harmonise and co-ordinate donor practices and procedures, and, as in other countries, making progress in this respect will require strong leadership from the Ministry of Finance. Without such an effort, as aid flows increase, donors will be placing an ever-increasing burden on government ministers and senior officials, as numbers of parallel reporting requirements, donor missions and local consultation committees expand. Possible approaches to this problem include: persuading more partners to channel support through the budget or sector baskets; establishing a well-spaced annual cycle of consultation meetings to rationalise interactions with local donor groups; declaring quiet times of the year for donor missions and establishing targets for reducing mission frequency; and on occasion being ready to say 'no' to aid offered in the wrong modalities or the wrong form. We strongly welcome and encourage the intention of the Ministry of Finance to work with development partners to put such arrangements in place in Malawi.

Implications for the MGDS and its implementation

Since this report coincided with the final stages of preparation of the new MGDS, which was due to replace the MPRS, it may be helpful to emphasise a few points we see as being key to the successful design and implementation of the MGDS.

Given the track record with the MPRS and limited financial management capacity in the Ministry of Finance (including the absence of a functioning medium-term expenditure framework), we hope the MGDS will be seen as a flexible medium-term strategy to be converted year-by-year into annual budgets. While it is right to try to cost the first year of implementation and to illustrate the full cost over time of major long-term capital projects, it would be a mistake to attach much weight to any costings developed for later years or to regard the MGDS as any kind of five-year expenditure plan. The uncertainties, both about what will be feasible or make practical sense as events unfold, and about future aid flows are too great. It would be more sensible to think in terms of various possible scenarios for future levels of expenditure, exploring what might be achieved under different scenarios.

While a national development strategy should be comprehensive, it is essential for Malawi to identify priorities for action. For example, if improving food security is a top priority for the immediate future, then the strategy should say so and should say what is to be done to achieve it, such as improving water harvesting and encouraging commercial farming. We think the strategy should also identify priority policy changes, some of which may have few expenditure implications, as well as expenditure priorities. While there was some attempt to define priorities and reduce the number of focus actions and priority activities in successive drafts of the MGDS that we saw, we are still concerned that this effort does not go far enough.

The government should put significant effort into explaining the Malawi Growth and Development Strategy to the general population and to those responsible for implementation at the local level. It is also important to engage parliament. We believe the strategy should be formally endorsed by parliament, either as a document supporting the annual budget process or through another mechanism.

The Ministry of Finance and Ministry of Economic Planning and Development (MEPD) need to work together to try to ensure that annual budgets and budget outturns are clearly and transparently linked to the MGDS. This will require effective arrangements for challenging ministries' budget bids and for monitoring and evaluating outturns.

It will take time to develop the trust needed for most development partners to direct a substantial proportion of their support through the budget. In the meantime, donors should be encouraged to direct less of their support into individual projects and more into sector strategies, through a series of sector SWAps building on the model established in the health sector. As noted above, this form of support has a number of advantages when capacity is weak.

We welcome the Ministry of Finance's intention to work with donors to seek to align their support behind the MGDS and to develop a programme for improved co-ordination and harmonisation of donor procedures and practices.

Lessons for other countries

There are a number of lessons from Malawi's experience that may be applicable in other countries that have encountered difficulties implementing first generation poverty reduction strategies. These are as follows:

- Even more than in countries where capacity is stronger, it is essential to use the strategy to identify a relatively limited set of achievable actions and expenditure priorities. This should be the strategy's focus. While actions in the first year need to be costed, it may be unrealistic to seek to set out anything resembling a medium-term expenditure plan. Instead, it may be more useful for the strategy to illustrate a range of medium-term scenarios, illustrating, for example, the progress that could be made with different levels or modalities of external assistance.

- The initial aim should be to try to ensure that annual budgets, as they are prepared and executed, are consistent with the strategy, and ministries of finance have a key role to play in challenging sector ministries' spending plans and ensuring plans when agreed are executed effectively.
- Outreach is important, to explain the strategy to the general public and to those responsible for implementation at a local level. So, too, is a process to engage parliament.
- Where confidence among development partners is weak, it may be more realistic to seek to establish arrangements where donors can channel funds into sector baskets – SWAps – rather than expecting a rapid move towards a more substantial measure of direct budget support.
- Strong government leadership can do much – and is usually welcomed by donors – to make progress in implementing in each country the global commitments that have been made to align donor support behind country strategies, and to co-ordinate and harmonise donor practices and procedures to reduce the administrative burden on government.

Finally, in a number of respects, Malawi is now demonstrating the power of learning from the experience of other countries and indeed, where appropriate, importing systems and procedures developed in other countries. We believe that governments can learn more from other governments in this respect than they are likely to learn from international institutions and other development partners.

Note

1. Chinyamata Chipeta is Professor of Economics, Chancellor College, University of Malawi.

CHAPTER 5

Monitoring Donor Support for the Poverty Reduction Strategy in Bangladesh: Rethinking the Rules of Engagement

Professor Wahiduddin Mahmud[1]

I   Introduction

The process of preparing a Poverty Reduction Strategy Paper (PRSP) was undertaken seriously in Bangladesh after a new government with a strong parliamentary majority was elected in October 2001. An interim PRSP (I-PRSP) entitled 'A national strategy for economic growth, poverty reduction and social development' was finalised in March 2003 (Government of Bangladesh [GOB], 2003). Earlier, an initial draft of the I-PRSP had been made available for discussions with various stakeholders including Bangladesh's development partners[2]. A much more extensive process of consultations was involved in moving from the I-PRSP to the full PRSP, a draft of which was produced in December 2004. Further rounds of consultations followed and the final version of the PRSP, entitled 'Unlocking the potential: national strategy for accelerated poverty reduction' was produced in October 2005 (GOB, 2005).

The timing of the finalisation of the I-PRSP was significant. Immediately following the preparation of the I-PRSP and its joint assessment by the World Bank and the IMF (World Bank, 2003), the government successfully applied for the IMF's programme lending under the so-called Poverty Reduction and Growth Facility (PRGF) and the World Bank's Development Support Credit (DSC) under the PRSP umbrella. Both these credit programmes were negotiated under a medium-term policy framework involving disbursements of funds in a series of instalments.

Subsequently, the full PRSP was also given a general nod of approval by the Bank-IMF joint assessment (World Bank, 2005). All other development partners, including the UN agencies, the Asian Development Bank (ADB) and bilateral donors, have in principle accepted the need for aligning their aid operations along the Poverty Reduction Strategy (PRS) approach, while also pursuing their agency-specific goals. This is reflected the recent donor policy statements, as articulated in the World Bank's Bangladesh Country Assistance Strategy 2006-2009, the ADB's Bangladesh Country Strategy and Programme for 2006-2010 and the United Nations Development Assistance Framework in Bangladesh 2006-2010, the latter being a joint document of the government and UN agencies in Bangladesh. Bilateral donors have also agreed more or less to follow the lead[3]. At the same time, donor agencies have also taken initiatives for harmonising and co-ordinating their aid operations in the country. Thus, at least in terms of their out-ward stance and declared policies, donors would appear to have committed themselves to the PRS process.

The purpose of this study is to examine how donor agencies in Bangladesh are responding to the new aid ideas and redefining their rules of engagement in support of the PRS process. The focus is not on the PRSP itself, but its preparation and implementation is discussed to the extent that it helps to understand the imperatives of the emerging aid modalities. Section II discusses the quality of the PRS process in Bangladesh in terms of its country ownership and policy contents. Section III first looks at the government's initiatives for PRS implementation and monitoring and then examines donors' responses to the PRS process. Section IV examines what donors can do differently in light of the lessons learnt from past experience and given a governance-challenged environment (as exists in Bangladesh). Section V provides some concluding remarks.

II   Quality of the Poverty Reduction Strategy

Ownership and participation

It is an undeniable fact that the Government of Bangladesh has undertaken the task of preparing the PRSP in order to remain eligible for soft loans from the World Bank and the IMF. It is ironic therefore that the issue of country 'ownership' itself has arisen as a matter of aid conditionality. While this is generally true of the PRSP process worldwide, the preparation of the I-PRSP in Bangladesh has been directly linked to accessing the Bank-IMF programme of assistance under a medium-term policy framework. This is likely to have worked against policy ownership at the very beginning of the PRSP process, since the policy agenda in the full PRSP is likely to have been pre-empted to some extent by the World Bank/IMF-supported policy framework.

Despite this, Bangladesh has had a long tradition of preparing five-year plans, the most recent one at the time of writing being the Fifth Five Year Plan for the period 1997–2002. It is true that enthusiasm for such plans has gradually eroded, because of their decreasing relevance in a market-oriented liberalised policy environment with the reduced role of public investment. In fact, the Fifth Five Year Plan represented an attempt to shift from quantitative investment allocations to strategic and policy planning[4]. Even as the idea of Five Year Plans went out of fashion following the rise of economic neoliberalism, expert opinion in the country remained in favour of having a well-articulated medium-term development strategy[5]. Therefore, in the absence of the Five Year Plans, the PRSP process in Bangladesh has a good chance of being seen as a continuation of a nationally owned planning process. Given the long tradition of state planning in the country, there is also likely to be political demand for the PRSP, even if that demand may in part be of a populist nature.

However, ownership is a complex issue. There is ownership by officials in the government ministries and by those responsible for implementation at the local level; national ownership as endorsed by the elected government and the parliament; ownership by stakeholders such as civil society and businesses; and ownership (or at least a degree of understanding of the strategy) among the general population. **There is also a crucial difference between ownership of PRSP preparation and that of its implementation.**

For example, is the participatory approach and openness to be continued beyond PRSP preparation to implementation? Will the government be willing to commit to a transparent and accountable process of monitoring? Clearly, the test of the government's commitment will be in implementation.

Ownership of PRSP in Bangladesh has been enhanced by the fact that the government has managed the process of its preparation entirely on its own, using local expertise and involving a participatory process. The I-PRSP was drafted by competent local experts from outside the government, but extensive consultations with various stakeholders had preceded its preparation[6]. Nonetheless, the transition from the I-PRSP to the full PRSP involved a far more extensive and structured consultations at the national, regional and local levels involving grassroots poor, non-government and community organisations, the private sector, trade unions, academia, research organisations and other community leaders.

The analytical inputs for the PRSP were provided by a number of thematic groups, which included researchers, development practitioners, government policy-makers and donor representatives[7]. **The incorporation of these inputs meant that the full PRSP took a more comprehensive and wider approach to its developmental strategy compared to the I-PRSP.** The formation of an inter-ministerial steering committee chaired by the principal secretary for the overall supervision of the PRSP process helped to ensure 'buy in' by government line agencies. Thus, while it is not easy to remove the perception that the PRSP is primarily linked to the provision of external support, there has clearly been an effort to establish it as the central national framework for growth and poverty reduction. This was signalled by shifting the 'home' of the PRSP from the Economic Relations Division (ERD) to the General Economics Division of the Planning Commission.

While the PRSP was officially approved by government, it was not debated in the national parliament, nor formally endorsed by it. Given the quality of debates in Bangladesh's parliament, such as on the annual budgets or other economic issues, it may be argued that not much of substance has been lost by this lapse in national ownership. Some discussions among MPs on the PRSP were arranged under a UNDP-sponsored project. While some donors pushed for parliamentary discussion of the PRSP, it would appear that the government did not want to expose the strategy to the country's confrontational party politics for pragmatic reasons. While it is difficult to deny the importance of parliamentary endorsement of the PRSP, at least for its symbolic value, it is unlikely that an incoming government would refuse to accept the PRSP process in some form or another.

The participatory approach adopted in the preparation of the PRSP is not new to Bangladesh. Back in the early 1990s, the country's Planning Commission undertook the enormous task of preparing a perspective plan for 1995–2010 using consultations at various levels – including grassroots-level participation[8]. Again, Bangladesh was one of the participating countries in the Structural Adjustment Participatory Review Initiative (SAPRI), which was launched in the late 1990s jointly by the World Bank, national governments and a global network of civil society organisations[9].

A participatory approach can give useful insights in assessing development policies and strategies, but it also has many limitations. Such an approach cannot be a substitute for the solid analytical work that is needed for economic policy-making. Economic policy reforms and their outcomes often involve inherently complex and interlinked processes, and uninformed discussions on these may lead to economic populism rather than rational choices. For example, the articulation of economic needs does not often relate to the resource constraint. However, the process can be beneficial in creating awareness about economic choices to be made and in obtaining insights from people's perceptions about ground-level realities. Some of the policy priorities of the PRSP, such as the need for better criminal justice, improved sanitation or maternal health care, may have arisen out of insights gained from grassroots consultations. **However, the greatest potential role of a participatory approach perhaps lies in its use as a mechanism of public accountability in the actual implementation of poverty reduction policies and strategies.**

Bangladesh's PRSP proposes many policies, particularly for improving the quality of governance, the implementation of which will be politically difficult. This problem is amply demonstrated by the discussion about how to find possible 'entry points' for solving governance-related problems. The PRSP thus at times gives the impression of telling the government what it should do rather than what the government actually proposes to do. This is to some extent inevitable in a document like this. The government is not monolithic, it has many faces. **The PRSP, or for that matter any such public document, relates to the part of the government that represents its so-called 'benevolent social guardian role', not the part that represents vested interests. The PRSP process, in this sense, is itself an entry point.**

The Poverty Reduction Strategy itself: is there a consensus on a development agenda?

The preparation of the Poverty Reduction Strategy Paper has benefited from the vast amount of development literature available on the development experience and prospects in Bangladesh. The development agenda of the PRSP is built on the policy triangle of pro-poor growth, human development and governance.

The strategy takes into account that the poverty impact of accelerated growth on per capita income since the early 1990s has been compromised to some extent by a worsening of income distribution[10]. Thus, while the focus of the PRSP is on private-sector-led development, it seeks ways of making development more inclusive and pro-poor. For example, its emphasis on supporting the development of a dynamic 'meso-economy' derives from evidence of the potential role of rural towns or 'growth centres' in generating productive employment opportunities in the informal and unorganised parts of the non-farm economy.

While the scope of the study that this chapter presents did not permit any detailed analysis of the envisaged development strategy of the PRSP, it is of interest to see how far it conforms to the standard Bank-IMF policy agenda. While giving a general nod of approval to the PRSP, the Bank-IMF joint assessment of it is also mildly critical about its certain aspects (World Bank, 2005). Thus, according to this assessment: the PRSP emphasises agricultural and rural development, but lacks a prioritised plan of actions within the resource and capacity constraint; it does not give enough prominence to the role of foreign direct investment; it proposes to provide direct support to private enterprises, although there are not many examples of such a sector-specific promotion strategy having worked; and it does not reflect the government's own roadmap for financial sector reforms, including the corporatisation and eventual privatisation of nationalised commercial banks, as already agreed under the Bank-IMF programme.

There may be, however, other credible criticisms of both the PRSP and its assessment by the Bank-IMF staffs. For example, the budgetary deficits are pre-fixed in the PRSP's medium-term macroeconomic framework, presumably to restrain the government from overspending, but this ignores the importance of flexibly managing an appropriate mix of fiscal, monetary and external reserve policies in light of evolving circumstances. Also, the concerns about budgetary deficits seem entirely to do with maintaining fiscal sustainability and macroeconomic stabilisation, although there is also an important issue involved here regarding an ideal mix of public-private investment. Again, while proposing further trade liberalisation through tariff reductions, the potential role of an industrial and trade policy to promote pro-poor growth is ignored. This role arises from the fact that the impact of tariff reforms is bound to vary across industries and sectors having varying potential for growth and poverty alleviation, so that if there is no well-devised industrial policy, there will be one by default[11]. As regards an appropriate state-market mix, the prevailing consensus seems to be that it should be decided not by pre-conceived ideas, but on the basis of evidence regarding what works best in the specific situations; however, there is less consensus on what that evidence is. The upshot of all this is that the PRSP should not give an impression, even if inadvertently, that there exists a consensus on a unique development roadmap; instead, its value should lie in its capacity to generate healthy debates on development alternatives facing Bangladesh. This will indeed be a test of ownership of its development agenda.

The PRSP has a very detailed set of what it calls 'policy matrices', covering macroeconomic management, sectoral policies and many cross-cutting development themes like governance, environmental sustainability, food security and women's rights. Each of the policy matrices shows the PRSP policy agenda for FY05–FY07, along with future priorities under different strategic goals, actions already taken or underway and the implementing government agencies. These policy matrices were a useful addition in moving from the I-PRSP to the final PRSP, since these represent an attempt to translate the PRS into a concrete action plan. As a tool for engagement with donors, the importance of such a policy agenda cannot be overemphasised. **The Paris Declaration stipulates that 'donors draw aid conditions, whenever possible, from the partner's national development strategy' and that 'other conditions would be included only when a sound justification exists' to act otherwise.**

At the risk of simplification, the numerous items in the policy agenda for 2005–07 can be divided into some generic categories (only some illustrative examples are given):

- **Specific actions for improved governance and an improved investment climate that may be politically resisted.** For example: improving public procurement processes such as through online tendering[12], separation of the judiciary from the executive, reducing the role of MPs in the development spending of local government bodies (e.g. *Union Parishads*), setting up a Human Rights Commission, reforming labour laws to prevent politicisation and establishing a private sea-port. It may be noted that enacting a law regarding right to information is included only under 'future priorities'.
- **Reiteration of qualitative assertions for improving governance without indicating how the goals will be achieved.** For example: making the Anti-corruption Commission effective and credible and generally strengthening the watchdog

bodies, enhancing efficient use of fiscal resources, enhancing reforms for revenue mobilisation, minimising losses from state-owned enterprise, improving the management of ports and customs clearance procedures, strengthening agricultural extension and improving the efficiency of safety-net measures. While some specific administrative measures are suggested, such as establishing a framework for fiscal reporting and control, the effectiveness of such measures remains an open question.

- **Programmes involving institutional innovations that will need further probing about what works and what does not.** For example: promoting private industrial estates, setting up a joint-venture investment-financing company under government sponsorship, setting up a loan-recovery agency, cost-effective designing of safety-net programmes, improving rural financing of non-farm activities, ensuring community input in designing local projects, support to agricultural marketing and development of more efficient irrigation, helping the growth of small-scale industries and creating an enabling environment for women to participate fully across a whole range of economic activities.

- **Setting up committees, conducting studies or collating results from piloting projects** regarding various development issues, such as: technology development and transfer, women's entrepreneurship, small and medium enterprise development and agricultural diversification.

- **Vague or unrealistic policies lacking the rigour of a strategic approach**, like providing access to electricity to 90 per cent of the population, and substantially increasing budgetary allocations every year for poverty alleviation and agricultural development.

- **Policy agenda already agreed under ongoing Bank-IMF programme lending.** For example, reforms of state-owned banks through management contracts, rationalising power tariffs and modernisation of the central bank. Much of the policy agenda for health and the population and for primary education is pre-empted by the ongoing donor-supported programmes based on a sector-wide approach (SWAp).

A few observations may be made about the above characteristics of the PRSP policy matrices. A basic thrust of the policy agenda is about finding an appropriate role for the government regarding how it can effectively help an essentially private-sector-led development process and how the quality of public services can be improved. There will be a need for a continuing assessment of that role; and this will need expert help from within and outside the government, as well as ground-level feedback. Some of the deficiencies of the policy matrices have arisen from the fact that these have been prepared by different ministries on a somewhat ad hoc basis, almost as an afterthought, whereas the text of the PRSP has benefited from inputs from several 'thematic groups', which included experts and researchers from outside the government. Not surprisingly, while the text of the PRSP articulates the issues well, the policy matrices that outline the action plans for implementation are not always consistent with the text and are often rather vague. **There is clearly a need to constitute advisory groups similar to the thematic groups in order to institutionalise the process of mobilising professional expertise in further articulation and implementation of the PRS.**

Reiterating the governance-related agenda (the first two of the above bulleted categories) is important in terms of government ownership, even if the feasibility of their effective implementation remains doubtful. In this regard, having a long 'wish list' may not help unless some priorities are indicated. This is also true for the desirable economic reforms that are likely to be resisted politically. It is the government, and not the donors, which can make a judgement about how to best practice the 'art of the feasible'. **By the World Bank's own admission, one of the lessons it has learned from its experience of aid operations in Bangladesh is that more attention needs to be given to the political realities of the country**[13]. This is one of the ways the World Bank is proposing to provide aid differently in Bangladesh. A prioritised agenda of reforms under the PRS can thus help to avoid unrealistic aid conditionality as well as promote policy ownership.

As mentioned above, the PRSP policy agenda is likely to have been pre-empted to some extent by the policy framework agreed under the Bank-IMF programme of lending. There is also the question of the mindset of government policy-makers, namely, their perception about what is expected of the PRSP. After all, the PRSP had to be approved by the Bank-IMF's respective boards. An illustrative example is provided by the PRSP policy matrix for the power sector. In line with the World Bank's general reform agenda, the policy matrix has avoided proposing the creation of any additional power generation capacity in the public sector. It is the World Bank that has now reassessed its policy stance in this regard, and in 2007 agreed to provide an International Development Association (IDA) loan of $275 million to set up a power plant under government ownership. A power generation company will be set up for this purpose and the plant will be run initially under management contract given out through international bidding. The Bank has come up with this idea particularly in view of the country's severe power shortage and the government's apparent lack of capacity to attract independent power companies. **Ironically, the World Bank appears to be more proactive than Bangladesh's government policy-makers in deviating from its own professed privatisation policies and finding an innovative state-market mix.**

The above comments are not intended to imply that the PRSP policy matrices are not useful. In fact, a large number of the proposed programmes and policies are conducive to promoting pro-poor growth. A particular contribution of the policy matrices is to point out that many development challenges need multi-pronged actions requiring inter-agency co-operation. The policy matrices also represent a useful stocktaking of the ongoing development activities of the government. Nonetheless, much more work is needed to translate these policy matrices into what the Paris Declaration calls 'prioritised result-oriented operational programmes'.

III   Implementation and monitoring of the PRS: the government's initiatives and donor responses

Monitoring mechanism for PRS implementation

Bangladesh's PRSP document gives a detailed account of the proposed systems for monitoring and evaluation regarding the implementation of the national development strategies. In fact, monitoring is regarded as one of the eight strategic agendas of the PRS, as it is seen to be performing multiple roles related to 'implementation, accountability, result-orientation and progress statement'. Like the policy matrices, the PRSP also includes monitoring matrices that show a detailed set of outcome or impact indicators related to input indicators (such as public spending or policy change) under various strategic goals. However, the list of indicators is said to be only 'a suggestive one and will need to be refined in the actual process of monitoring'[14].

If monitoring has to serve multiple purposes, it has to be based on different approaches – and these cannot be always translated into a uniform format of input-outcome indicators as shown in the PRSP. The broad development indicators, such as those related to poverty reduction or human development, are important to assess whether enough progress is being made towards achieving the overall PRS goals. To ensure accountability, the emphasis needs to be on reviewing public financial management and budgetary accounting mechanisms. However, there are also various impact assessment methods for evaluating the effectiveness of particular policies or programmes.

It is not easy to develop 'simple-yet-comprehensive' assessment tools and methodologies that will satisfy all participants. Fortunately, there are plenty of studies already available regarding the impact of various development programmes in Bangladesh, and it will be helpful for PRS monitoring to initially perform a stocktake of these studies. For example, many programmes, such as rural works programmes, have a track record of successfully targeting the intended beneficiaries; in these cases the monitoring emphasis should be on how to prevent the alleged leakage of funds. Programmes for providing mother-and-child health care have been found to have a beneficial pro-poor impact; in this case the monitoring of effectiveness needs to focus on whether the uptake of these services can be improved, possibly through more effective awareness campaigns[15]. Again, the evidence already gathered from many existing piloting programmes can be used to conduct *ex ante* impact assessment for the replication of such programmes on a larger scale. This kind of evidence can also be used to incorporate in-built monitoring mechanisms into the project design, such as through community participation and surveillance.

The Paris Declaration emphasises the need for translating development strategies into 'prioritised results-oriented operational programmes' and relating these programmes to 'annual budgets and medium-term expenditure frameworks'. This is a tall order, both conceptually and in practical terms. Bangladesh's PRSP has a medium-term macroeconomic framework, which consists of a three-year rolling plan. Unlike the previous five-year plans, the idea of a rolling plan provides scope for annual reviews to make the necessary adjustments in macroeconomic management. In addition, the Planning Commission is to see that the projects and programmes included in the rolling plan can 'act as a vehicle for operationalising the PRSP'[16]. At the same time, the line ministries are to be given more autonomy to align their programmes to the PRS under a medium-term budget framework (MTBF). Accordingly, at the time of the presentation of the national annual budget for FY07, the Ministry of Finance prepared a MTBF document containing an analysis of the 'medium-term budget strategy' for the period FY07–FY09 as well as the budgetary plans of ten line ministries for the same period (Government of Bangladesh, 2006).

While the above arrangements look promising on paper, there are several risks. The size of each Annual Development Plan (ADP) is revised downward almost routinely towards the end of every financial year, for reasons of both resource shortfall and problems of project implementation. Besides adversely affecting development-spending priorities, this also results in time and cost overruns in project implementation. The same problem may persist in the implementation of the MTBF as well. **It is also alleged that** the ministries have no incentive to implement the MTBF, as they would lose their existing discretionary authority. There is also lack of expertise in the line ministries for implementing the MTBF, and on top of this is the problem of retaining the trained personnel (the latter is cited as a major problem in donors' efforts to assist the training of government officials). At the same time, the Planning Commission does not have the expertise to scrutinise projects according to the PRS priorities, which would have been a demanding task to perform anyway, even with properly skilled staff. Finally, there are well-known adverse political incentives that are liable to distort public spending priorities[17]. While a number of co-ordinating committees are already in place to oversee the implementation of the MTBF, the effectiveness of these committees has yet to be tested[18].

Budget monitoring is not generally effective in Bangladesh because of the weakness of the country's accounting and auditing procedures, delays in expenditure reporting and the ineffectiveness of parliament's Public Accounts Committee. A key element of PRS monitoring will, therefore, have to involve a strengthening of budgetary accounting mechanisms relating to auditing, public procurement and the tracking of expenditure to show the use of funds. **Among other things, this would need 'timely, transparent and reliable reporting on budget execution', to quote from the Paris Declaration.**

An analysis of the trends in the broad budgetary allocations in Bangladesh over the years shows that patterns of public spending have been generally in concordance with the government's declared development strategy, namely, to promote private-sector-led growth while also attempting to alleviate poverty and promote social development (Mahmud, 2002). Thus, not only have the proportions of public spending in social sectors like health and education increased, but also the emphasis within these sectors is found to be on those expenditures that have a relatively pro-poor impact, such as on essential health care and primary education. **However, the problem with public development spending starts to appear only when one looks at the quality of project design and implementation.** It is generally recognised that there has been a huge wastage of public resources due to poor project implementation and allegedly large leakages of funds.

The weakness of the budgetary process arises to a large extent from its often piecemeal and fragmented approach, without its being linked to a strategic framework. It is in this respect that the effective implementation and monitoring of the PRS will have to make a difference. There is an acute shortage of expertise, as well as lack of incentive in ministries and planning agencies to prepare well-designed development projects. A centralised technocratic approach, without any mechanism of feedback through beneficiary participation, has also proved to be a major impediment in ensuring project outcomes are beneficial to local communities. There is little incentive or demand within the government system to come up with well-designed projects or programmes. A recent evaluation on rehabilitation of some of the projects of the Bangladesh Water Development Board shows that the original purpose of the projects was vindicated by more than 80 per cent of the people in the respective localities, but only one out of the 35 projects could be successfully rehabilitated. Among many problems, neglect of the details of local circumstances was found to be the main cause of failure (Mahmud, 2002a).

An elaborate institutional framework has been proposed to monitor PRS implementation. The existing National Steering Committee formed to overview the PRSP preparation will also be responsible for reviewing the progress of PRS implementation. In addition, a National Poverty Focal point has been established at the General Economics

Division (GED) of the Planning Commission for the necessary documentation relating to PRS implementation. A Technical Committee composed of the top officials from the Planning Commissions and other related ministries, as well as technical experts, will monitor the consistency of projects and programmes with the PRS goals[19]. A number of working groups, consisting of government and donor officials, experts and practitioners, have been formed around the ministries similar to the PRSP's thematic groups. Finally, the government has recently formed a high-profile independent advisory committee consisting of experts, researchers and civil society leaders to provide guidance and advice and to commission studies for an annual assessment of the progress made towards Poverty Reduction Strategy implementation and the attainment of the Millennium Development Goals (MDGs).

Concerns have been raised about lack of capacity and manpower in the ministries to carry out the additional work of monitoring and evaluation. Involving outside experts and research organisations is, therefore, seen to be a key element of PRS monitoring, but the effectiveness of such an arrangement will depend to a large extent on the political will of the government and its 'ownership' of the PRS process. **It is one thing to involve independent experts through the thematic committees to prepare the PRSP, it is altogether another thing to involve such experts in the actual project design or in scrutinising the project implementation process.** The reluctance of the government to do away with the existing Official Secrecy Act also casts some doubt about how far the government will be willing to open up its budgetary operations for independent experts to monitor. **Given the powerful vested interests that tend to lose out as a result of improved governance of public spending, support for PRSP monitoring may be found wanting as implementation proceeds.** It may also be seen from the above discussion that monitoring involves different kinds of activities at different levels and thus needs a multi-track approach; relying on a single monitoring architecture, however elaborate, may not be adequate on its own. Further, there is a risk that the monitoring exercise is geared primarily only to satisfy the donors.

Donors' response in supporting the PRS process

As indicated earlier, Bangladesh's development partners generally agree on the need to align their overall support to the country – in terms of country strategies, policy dialogues and development funding programmes – on the basis of the PRS approach. There is much less agreement about how to achieve such alignment, particularly when it comes to the details of aid modalities. One overriding concern of the donors is about the perceived low 'aid absorptive capacity' of the country due to weak governance. There are frequent aid cancellations and a large part of committed aid remains unutilised[20]. Thus, helping Bangladesh to overcome governance-related constraints has become at least as important a donor concern as meeting resource needs for actual investment programmes. Whether there is any consensus among the donor community about how best to provide aid in such a governance-challenged environment is another matter (to be discussed later in this study).

The co-ordination of aid at the national level is undertaken in Bangladesh by a local consultative group, which organises plenary meetings and includes a number of sector-specific sub-groups. While in principle government's participation is welcome, co-ordination remains very much donor-driven and government representation in the

consultative process is generally weak and ineffective. To strengthen the quality of implementation of donor-funded development activities, an Aid Governance Initiative was
launched in 2003 by the donor agencies in partnership with the Government of
Bangladesh, which subsequently resulted in the adoption of some new policies, particularly in respect of government procurement procedures. It is noteworthy that the initiative was in response to donors' concerns regarding government accountability and its
efficiency of aid utilisation, and was not primarily about co-ordination of those donors'
own aid modalities[21].

More recently, a framework of collaboration between the government and donors,
called the Bangladesh Harmonisation Action Plan, has been prepared to implement the
pledges of the Rome and Paris Declarations: promoting the implementation of country-
owned PRS, harmonisation and alignment of aid to PRS, results-orientation of aid and
mutual accountability. The Action Plan appears impressive as it lays out in detail time-
bound actions and desired outcomes towards achieving the above goals; however, a
closer look at its contents also reveals the difficulty of implementation. Its value perhaps
lies more in a diagnosis of the problems than in finding ways of solving them.

One goal of aid harmonisation is to rely more on the government's own systems in
terms of (for example) procurement, financial management and reporting and adopting
joint-supervision strategies. One major problem lies in harmonising reporting and auditing requirements. In 2003, a new public procurement regulation was introduced by
the government largely following guidelines of the World Bank, which was to be used
uniformly across all public agencies. Donors still remain sceptical about the regulation's
effectiveness and think that further improvements will be needed to plug the loopholes.
As a result, the government has still to comply with a multiplicity of donors' procurement guidelines. Even when government systems are used, these are not relied on and
are often supplemented by additional work. The ADB and the World Bank, for example,
uses in some cases local private firms to audit their projects. The auditing standards
required by different donors vary to a large extent, thus giving confusing signals[22]. Nor
does adopting a sector-wide approach (SWAp) help; the ongoing SWAp in the primary
education sector, called PEDP-II, is known for its reliance on Bangladesh's own systems;
yet despite this, it still has to comply with six different procurement rules[23].

The perception of weak governance along with fiduciary and other risks inhibits
donors from using Bangladesh's own country systems, leading to the creation of parallel
implementation structures and excessive fragmentation of donor activities. Nor does
adopting a multi-donor programme-based approach always help, as will be seen in the
later discussion of this chapter on the health sector's SWAp. Donors complain about
the difficulty of finding enough capable or trustworthy officials within government agencies
to set up a programme with ownership. This lack of trust leads to a tendency for donors
to try to micro-manage their aid-financed projects, and to field too many project apprais-
als and performance review missions.

The Bangladesh Harmonisation Action Plan mentioned above does recognise the
need for reducing the administrative burden on the government by reducing the number of donor missions. It also proposes to field missions in line with the government's
monitoring requirements and to simplify annual portfolio review processes. In recent
years, the government's Economic Relations Division (ERD) received about 250 missions annually[24]. Donors have also often fielded parallel missions for the same purpose.
Repeated donor missions to study the development problems of the Chittagong Hill

Tracts (an area which has the country's largest concentration of tribal populations) are a case in point.

Consultations with donors take up an inordinate amount of government officials' time. To reduce this burden, possible approaches tried elsewhere include: establishing a regular and well-spaced annual cycle of consultation meetings and declaring 'quiet' periods in the year; avoiding parallel missions and sharing of the results of mission findings among relevant donors; specialisation among donor representatives according to expertise, so that not all donors need to be represented in the same meetings, particularly in the case of SWAps; **and for the government to be able on occasion to say 'no' to aid of the wrong kind or offered in the wrong modalities.**

All donors have taken the official position of aligning their aid operations to the PRSP. As mentioned earlier, this position has been explicitly stated in the country-assistance strategies (CASs) of multilateral and major bilateral donors and UN agencies. These country-assistance strategies have also been agreed with the government, and in the case of the UN agencies, produced jointly with the government. Further, as a step towards donor co-ordination and harmonisation, the World Bank has prepared its new CAS jointly with the ADB, the UK's Department for International Development (DFID) and Japan (*Bangladesh Country Assistance Strategy 2006–2009*). These four development partners – the 'big four' or 'the gang of four' as they are referred to by the smaller donors – together currently deliver $1 billion to $1.5 billion annually in gross aid to Bangladesh, well over 80 per cent of all development assistance to the country. In addition to the joint CAS of the World Bank, each of the other partners has their own separate strategy document as well[25].

An important part of the World Bank's joint CAS is an 'outcomes matrix' showing the expected outcomes and intermediate indicators or milestones, together with all the interventions supported by the four CAS partners relating to a given outcome. This implies a common assessment of the PRSP by the four partners based on an agreed common set of outcome indicators and a common understanding of the strategies needed to deliver these outcomes[26]. The strategies relate to the PRSP's longer-term development agenda, while the outcomes have considerable similarity with the PRSP's policy agenda matrices, discussed earlier. As expected, however, the PRSP covers a much wider range of strategies and policies than the CAS does, and the time frame is also a bit different – the PRSP's medium-term policy agenda was for the three-year period of FY05–FY07 while the 'outcomes/milestones' of the CAS refers to the four-year period of FY06–FY09.

While the alignment between the joint CAS and the PRSP appears promising, most of the PRSP strategic goals are broad enough for a range of policy agenda to fit in. **Nor is it clear that in every instance the policy agenda in the CAS is guided by that of the PRSP and not the other way round.** As discussed earlier, there is a degree of disjoint between the text and the policy matrices of the PRSP and some of the policies may have been pre-empted by ongoing Bank-IMF programme lending[27]. Most of the policies relating to governance and the investment climate are also common to both the documents; so they share some of the shortcomings of the PRSP policy agenda discussed earlier: either they are specific actions without prioritisation in terms of political feasibility, or they are of a qualitative nature without enough clues about which actions will actually deliver and which will not.

In some key governance issues, however, there are some apparently minor but significant differences between the PRSP policy agenda and the CAS milestones. Both include enactment of law regarding right to information, but the PRSP puts this under 'future priorities' only. Again, regarding the improvement of government procurement procedures, both go for almost similar actions, including the introduction of e-procurement; **however, the CAS agenda goes one crucial step further to include compliance with procurement regulations to be monitored 'through independent annual procurement review' and through civil society surveillance** (World Bank, 2006, p.107).

While the output indicators in the PRSP monitoring and evaluation matrices are of qualitative (and admittedly tentative) nature, the joint CAS has in some cases more concrete outcomes or milestones; however, this only shows the complexity in the choice of an appropriate outcome indicator. Thus, one of the milestones in the strategy of providing greater access to health services is to raise the share of the poorest 50 per cent of households in the delivery of essential health services from 55 per cent to 65 per cent (World Bank, 2006, p.101). This is only a partial indicator, if at all, in making health service provision more pro-poor. Since essential health services (including mother–child health care) are the only part of public health care that is found to be pro-poor, increasing the uptake of such services (even with an unchanged pattern of benefit incidence) will definitely be a pro-poor policy (Osmani, 2006; World Bank, 2003)[28]. **This is only illustrative of the much bigger problem of agreeing to a result-oriented modality of aid arrangements.**

Looking at the broad strategies or qualitative policy directions does not tell one much about whether the implementation of the PRSP will require donors to do things differently. These strategies are mostly broad and non-specific enough for the usual donor-funded projects and programmes to be able to pass the test anyway. What really matters, besides specific policy reforms, is the way these projects and programmes are conceived, designed and implemented[29]. So far as project aid is concerned, this is where the key to the issue of improving aid effectiveness through promoting 'ownership' lies, and the situation in this respect is far less encouraging. **As one donor official admitted: the effect of the PRSP on donors' modes of operation in this respect is minimal, it is 'business as usual'.** The criteria for judging the effectiveness of budgetary support, such as those provided by the World Bank's policy-based lending, are of course a different matter and will be discussed later.

Project aid, which accounts for the bulk of all aid to Bangladesh, has in recent years accounted for about one-third of the government's total development spending under the Annual Development Plan (ADP)[30]. The proportion of allocations to aid-assisted projects is of course much higher, because of the use of local funds in these projects. This proportion will also increase with the introduction of more SWAps.

Officials of donor agencies complain that government agencies do not have the competence to articulate the country's aid needs and prepare aid-worthy project proposals[31]. There is even less capability to prepare projects so as to fit into an overall or sectoral strategy framework. The result is various donors doing various things, resulting in aid fragmentation. Often donors do not know what to do with their funds[32]. When donor agencies come up with projects or programmes in areas that need a co-ordinated approach by many agencies – like the development of small and medium enterprises (SMEs) or supporting the rural non-farm sector – they even face difficulty in finding a 'home' for their project in the government. The nature of the challenge in solving these problems has already been discussed in relation to PRS implementation.

What can the donors do to improve the situation? While it is largely true that government agencies lack capability, the way donors prepare their project proposals often leaves much room for improvement. **In addition, donor-designed projects usually have the characteristics of a top-down approach that is inadequately informed by local knowledge of what works and what does not** (this problem will be discussed in detail below). Donor agencies also tend to push the aid agenda of their headquarters, or apply global templates in designing projects without adequate feedback about local cultural traditions and institutional characteristics. The extent of the problem depends on the complexity of the project, and on the analytical capacity and the autonomy of the aid agencies' local offices.

The World Bank, for example, has arguably the best analytical capability and has the strongest local presence, but it has elaborate project-implementation procedures involving the staff at its headquarters or even regional offices. DFID and the ADB have competent local staffs, as well as a fair degree of autonomy. The options for the smaller bilateral aid agencies are perhaps to pool resources with other donors within SWAps, or to pursue relatively simple projects with a proven track record. As will be argued later, hiring expatriate consultants can hardly compensate for having in-house analytical capacity. As for the UN agencies, they normally pursue projects in line with their global mandates and using their worldwide experience, but their projects may be handicapped where adaptation to local conditions are needed (see some examples below).

It is now recognised that donors can improve their aid efforts by engaging with civil society and by encouraging inputs from local experts. Donors usually engage in consultations with various local stakeholders to get feedback on their country-assistance strategies[33]. However, these consultations are not usually intended to obtain inputs for the design of specific projects. One of the 'lessons learned', as mentioned in the World Bank's CAS, is the need for a 'good local fit' for projects based on knowledge of local institutional capabilities and other ground realities (World Bank, 2006, p.63). Local experts could have predicted long before donors that the SWAp in Bangladesh's health sector, called HPSP, would not work because it was over-designed in terms of both institutional arrangements and resource needs (Mahmud and Mahmud, 2000). An unpublished completion report on the World Bank's CAS (FY01–FY04) found that most of the aid cancellations had been due to the need for project restructuring, pointing to the fact that the original project designs had lacked realism and institutional contextualisation[34]. There is a clear need for much deeper investigation than is possible through the routine, usual format project consultations.

There are some examples of how such investigation can help project design. The World Bank's recently approved project for community-driven local governance – a theme much emphasised in Bangladesh's Poverty Reduction Strategy Paper – is one such initiative[35]. Local governance has been on the priority list of reforms for a long time and the UNDP and other donor agencies have been piloting some projects in this area, providing the building blocks for larger-scale replication. The World Bank's project has been designed to place block grants at the disposal of the *Union Parishads* to be spent through community participation. The risks are there, particularly regarding fiduciary accountability and capture by local elite; however, the risks are being sought to be addressed by designing the project carefully through intimate interactions with the implementing government agencies, stakeholders and knowledgeable persons, as well as by taking advantage of the experience of previous pilot projects. In doing so, getting feedback – for instance, through brainstorming sessions and involving civil society leaders in the design and monitoring of the project – can do much more than setting up an elaborate formal structure of a project support unit staffed by expatriate experts. This consultative process should continue into the project implementation phase as well, so that there is a 'learning-by-doing' process in place and a visible mechanism of public accountability. Designing such a project, of course, requires a lot of initiative and imagination on the part of donor officials.

Another example is the proposed DFID-led project called PROSPER, which is aimed at supporting the development of micro-enterprises – again an area of emphasis in the PRSP[36]. The project will provide funds for scaling-up of micro-enterprises, thus trying to fill in the so-called 'missing middle' between micro-credit and formal bank lending. This is a challenging task involving risks, and the project proposal has been revised several times through consultations among local aid officials and key stakeholders, policymakers and practitioners in this field. In contrast, an International Finance Corporation-funded initiative, called SEDF[37], which is aimed at supporting SME development, has yielded very few tangible results beyond holding high-profile seminars and workshops; this is a project run by expatriate consultants with few effective interactions with local stakeholders. This initiative's current mode of knowledge management seems unsuitable for the task given to it: finding effective institutional arrangements for promoting private-sector development. However, the World Bank Group has now launched a multi-donor project for private-sector development (the PSD Support Project) which looks more promising because of its close attention towards interacting with government agencies, building local capacity and understanding stakeholder interests and positions.

While donors can improve their project design by incorporating the insights of local experts and practitioners, the process can be taken even one step further, namely, by offering assistance to government agencies for preparing the projects themselves. Government agencies can thus access to the same sources of expertise and knowledge, including the expertise of donor agency officials, and this will be in line with the true PRSP notion of 'ownership'.

One problem in such an arrangement is incentive incompatibility within donor agencies. Donor agency officials taking the initiative may not like to be denied their claim on the 'ownership' of the project idea. This only confirms the complexity of the notion of ownership. On the government's side, there is the usual reluctance or lack of initiative to use outside expertise to prepare innovative project designs. Another problem is that although reform-minded agencies and elements within government would welcome certain reforms that involve deviations from prevalent official practices, they either cannot put such reforms into the project design without going through a lengthy process of government approval or they may not want to be seen to be the advocates of such changes.

However, there are ways for both sides to meet halfway. Donors can help government agencies to propose the projects, leaving aside some difficult reform components; donors can then add these components during their appraisal as conditionality or 'assurances' to be given by the government (the SWAp in primary education, PEDP-II, has 33 such assurances). On the other hand, government officials can put forward some aspects of the project design that they genuinely believe to be beneficial for the project, but about which donors need to be convinced. This arrangement has the added benefit of the donor agency officials being able to apply better judgment and more flexibility in interpreting the guidelines of their headquarters, because they are only reacting to a proposal of the government.

At the time of writing, almost all monitoring and evaluation of donor assistance in Bangladesh was carried out by donors themselves, raising the question: who will monitor the donors? One of the key commitments made in the Paris Declaration is about 'mutual accountability' between donors and the partner country. The government's Economic Relations Division (ERD), which is supposed to be the gatekeeper for aid inflows, has very little capacity for such monitoring; it looks into some general rules and procedures for aid negotiations only and does not have the confidence and capability to demand what frameworks or modalities for aid negotiations will best suit the country's needs. The government needs to have a complete picture of donor activities in the country (which involves reporting obligations on the part of donors) and should be able to provide leadership in harmonising and co-ordinating donor practices and procedures. Any exchange of experiences of systems and procedures established in other developing countries could be helpful, and the government could perhaps learn more from other beneficiary countries in this respect than from its development partners.

According to the Paris Declaration, donor countries need to link their aid programming to the partner country's performance assessment frameworks, refraining from requesting the introduction of performance indicators that are not consistent with the PRS. In this respect, the effectiveness of the proposed PRSP monitoring process will be crucial. While the annual or periodic reviews of progress in PRSP implementation will be primarily needed for the sake of managing the country's overall development efforts, such reviews can also be a basis for result-oriented of aid negotiation. The newly established Poverty Monitoring Unit at the Planning Commission can also act as a depository of knowledge regarding donor activities, particularly since there is a lack of institutional memory on the part of donors in this respect.

IV What can donors do differently and how?

Changing aid ideas: providing aid in a governance-challenged environment

Aid ideas have changed over the years, partly in line with changing aid faddism, but partly in response to genuine assessment regarding aid effectiveness. The concern for making aid a vehicle for poverty alleviation has always been there, even when aid was viewed primarily as a means for resource transfer to support economic development. However, the experience of stabilisation and structural adjustment in the 1980s raised concerns about possible marginalisation of the poor and led to a reassessment of the role of the state, at least to give a 'human face' to market-oriented economic reforms. Subsequently, a broad consensus on goals for poverty alleviation and social development emerged in the 1990s in the form of the Millennium Development Goals (MDGs). Simultaneously, the emphasis moved from quantity to quality of development assistance, arising from the belief that in the past much assistance had been wasted by recipient countries. This new emphasis fits well with the 'modified' version of the so-called Washington consensus, which now incorporates institution-building and good governance as essential ingredients of the reform agenda. The PRSP process emphasising country ownership of reforms needs to be seen as the latest addition to these evolving aid ideas.

Over the years, development assistance to Bangladesh has been largely affected by these changing ideas. Thus the emphasis of aid has shifted to service delivery for the poor and infrastructure provision for rural development (Mahmud, 2002a). Notwithstanding this shift in the aid portfolio, the overriding donor concern regarding Bangladesh is how to best assist the country address its governance challenges. The underlying assumption is that weakness of the country's economic and political governance institutions reduces its aid absorptive capacity and keeps economic performance below its potential.

However, responses to the governance problem vary among donors, in spite of their efforts to give uniform signals. Small bilateral donors have very little leverage in demanding better governance, while their aid headquarters go by the overall governance signals coming out of the country[38]. Moreover, they have the option to confine their aid operations to relatively narrow areas of their choice, or can reduce the size of their country aid portfolio and shift aid funds to another country. For example, Bangladesh used to be the largest recipient of Danish aid worldwide in the early 1990s, but since then the country has been relegated to sixth or seventh position.

Large donors such as the 'big four' (the World Bank, ADB, Japan and DFID) tend to have a different perspective. Because of their relatively large aid portfolios, they have a larger stake in the country's overall economic performance and they can exercise enough leverage in the area of policy reforms by engaging with the government effectively. However, their approaches have hardly been consistent over the years. The World Bank's volume of assistance to Bangladesh, for example, has gone through troughs and peaks, which have much to do with shifts in the Bank's strategy on how to deal with the country's governance problem. Thus, immediately before Development Support Credits (DSCs) could be provided to Bangladesh in FY03, the Bank's aid pipeline to the country had become thin because of the its increasing disengagement from a large number of sectors, including infrastructure and energy, where progress in policy reforms had been lacking. More recently, however, the World Bank has shifted its stance in favour of working from within critical sectors, rather than disengaging from them while waiting for reforms to occur.

To determine performance-based allocations of IDA loans, the World Bank uses a numerical country-rating system based on its Country Policy and Institutional Assessment (CPIA). Overtime, the assessment criteria have shifted from a largely macroeconomic focus to include more and more governance-related indicators; as a result, the governance factor has now become the predominant determinant of country allocations. The CPIA has been criticised by experts for the excessive weight it places on governance, which puts countries like Bangladesh at a disadvantage. However, in spite of its low ratings, Bangladesh has not been able to fully access its IDA allocations because of the problem of identifying enough 'viable' projects[39]. The challenge for Bank officials and the government lies in finding aid modalities that can enable the country to fully utilise these allocations, while also trying to improve the country's CPIA rating. Contrary to common perception, the Bank's portfolio performance in Bangladesh has been found to be better than the average of South Asian (or that of IDA-only) countries in respect of the per cent of project at risk or of completed projects with satisfactory outcomes[40].

By providing budgetary support through DSCs, the World Bank has now been able to engage with the Bangladesh government across a much wider range of policy reforms. From the donors' point of view, the logic of providing budgetary support in a governance-challenged environment rests on the premise that the risk of misuse of additional funds will be more than compensated for by an improvement in the overall quality of resource management. Nonetheless, there is a danger of underestimating the political constraints while proposing a long list of reforms. According to the World Bank's own assessment, the three-year reform programme proposed in the DSC did not reflect a realistic analysis of institutional constraints and implementation capacity, which made it unlikely that the programme could be followed through completely[41].

In proposing governance-related institutional reforms, donors need to be patient and opportunistic instead of having a preconceived ideal design. This needs flexibility in the donor-supported reform agenda, particularly in determining the time-bound 'milestones' or indicators of progress. **As is rightly pointed out in the PRSP, there needs to be a continuous search for appropriate 'entry points' to bring about incremental, but strategic, changes in governance systems.** For example, the enactment of laws to make public procurement more accountable or to promote the right to information can potentially make a big difference across the board, although a law's initial effectiveness may be compromised by vested interests trying to get around it. Many donor-supported institutional reforms could produce results only after a prolonged period of experimentation. One example is the reduction in energy pilferage following the corporatisation of Dhaka's power supply authority[42].

Donor support for improving the institutions of governance can hardly be effective unless there is a local demand for such support. Donor support can only be complementary to the government's own efforts in implementing reforms in governance, such as those proposed in the PRSP. Lessons should be learnt from the more than 100 donor-supported projects that are being implemented, covering areas such as policing, justice or anti-corruption. While donor support towards good governance is encouraging, the effectiveness of the above types of projects needs careful scrutiny.

The record of donors' efforts to build or support good sector-level institutions has been largely disappointing, except for a few 'islands of excellence' such as in microfinance (PKSF), rural infrastructure (LGED) and rural electrification (REB)[43]. In each of these cases, there was a confluence of many factors contributing to the success of the respective institutions, such as strong leadership along with autonomy and ownership, which provided a kind of 'ring-fencing' from adverse outside interferences. There is also no guarantee that the so-called islands of excellence will continue to remain so. The REB, for example, recently suffered serious setbacks because of politicisation of its rural co-operatives; however, the rot is alleged to have really started from the top, with changes in its leadership.

Appropriate designing of projects is important in addressing governance concerns. One way is to build into project design mechanisms of accountability, through, for example, contracting out services to the private sector, fostering collaboration between government agencies and NGOs and encouraging beneficiary participation; there are recent examples of these mechanisms being applied successfully in Bangladesh. Again, donors face the problem of 'moral hazard' in project design as they try to reduce aid-delivery costs by relying on government systems, while also addressing their legitimate concerns about leakage of funds due to corruption. An appropriate balance may be achieved by emphasising the mitigation of the fiduciary risks (through auditing and financial reporting), while avoiding micro-managing the projects through too many project-support units.

There have been frequent cancellations of aid to ongoing projects and premature termination of projects. **Public monitoring of mutual accountability would be greatly served if donors and the government could agree to make the reasons of such actions public.** It would help to create more awareness of the factors that adversely affect aid effectiveness, and could thus better inform public discourse on the subject. After all, it is the ordinary people of Bangladesh who stand to lose out most from any act of malfeasance in aid utilisation.

Some donors have preferred the NGO route for aid delivery, given the strong presence of NGOs in Bangladesh and their long experience in service delivery and community-based activities. For example, the United States Agency for International Development (USAID) currently delivers almost 90 per cent of aid through NGOs, European Union 45 per cent and DFID 25 per cent. While total grant aid to Bangladesh has been declining, the share going to NGOs has increased rapidly – from 11 per cent out of US$938 million in 1990–91 to 45 per cent out of US$690 million in 2003–04 (Bangladesh Bank, 2006, p.151). In this respect donors face a dilemma: on the one hand, given the inefficiencies of the government machinery, NGOs can be used for effective delivery of basic services; on the other, this approach is liable to have a disabling effect for donor agencies when engaging in the debate regarding governance and public service delivery. There is also an increasing recognition of the need for government–NGO partnerships and for ensuring better accountability of NGOs, through, for example, strengthening local governance. It is important that donors co-ordinate their efforts in this area and do not act at cross purposes.

Recent changes in aid ideas, discussed earlier, have not always been entirely beneficial to aid effectiveness. **The shift of emphasis to poverty alleviation may have given rise to a kind of 'aid populism': aid has to be seen to be used for poverty alleviation.** As directly targeted poverty interventions, including service delivery for the poor have been emphasised, so investments in key areas like infrastructure, energy and technology development have remained underfunded. While this shift was clearly visible in the World Bank's global aid portfolio, this was accentuated in case of the Bank's operations in Bangladesh for reasons mentioned above. This situation was, however, compensated to some extent by the two other large donors, the ADB and Japan, continuing to remain engaged in the above sectors.

There has been yet another more recent shift of donor emphasis in terms of promoting human rights and good governance through NGO-led community mobilisation. Donor funding has undoubtedly played the key role in enabling NGOs to deliver effective services in such areas as basic health, informal education and micro-credit. Whether donor-funded NGO initiatives can be equally effective in the above new areas of emphasis is yet to be tested. It is difficult to find measurable indicators to monitor the success of such initiatives; and this makes the problem of NGO accountability even more difficult. Moreover, since such activities can often take on the character of campaigns of a political nature, funding by donors may become a contested issue.

Using local knowledge more, and technical assistance discriminatingly

The importance of incorporating local knowledge into project design has already been discussed. The fact that aid-funded projects and programmes remain primarily donor-driven and are prepared by donor agencies often limits the scope of their benefiting from intimate and grassroots-level knowledge of local conditions. This is a major problem in making aid programmes more locally relevant, institutionally feasible and cost-effective. A few examples from Bangladesh's recent experience in this regard can amply illustrate this point.

First, donors may have a tendency to go for the universally accepted ideal technology, ignoring a lower-cost intermediate technology that will be more readily adopted by local communities. In order to improve rural sanitation in Bangladesh, the Public Health Engineering Department was supported by UNICEF to promote water-sealed, fully sanitary latrines. However, a lower-cost but usable technology of ring-slab latrines promoted by local entrepreneurs, combined with creating awareness about the value of better hygiene, has proved to be a much more effective means of improving sanitation at the initial stage. This is a solution based on knowledge of what can be best achieved in the local conditions[44].

Second is the example of a programme supported the UN Population Fund (UNFPA) and the World Health Organization (WHO) to train young women as skilled birth attendants (SBAs), which is cited by many local experts as a case of policy failure[45]. This programme is alleged to have bypassed the task of technically upgrading the more culturally experienced traditional birth attendants (TBAs) located within the communities. The result is that the newly trained, inexperienced SBAs find very little demand for their services[46].

UN agencies like UNFPA and UNICEF allegedly tend to ignore the importance of low-cost local solutions for reducing the maternal mortality rate (MMR), because of their global mandate to use the services of skilled birth attendants. Survey results, for example, show that there is ample scope for creating awareness about utilising existing institutional capacities for antenatal care as a means of screening potentially complicated deliveries, thereby reducing the MMR. Meanwhile, creating awareness of low-cost solutions is one thing that Bangladesh does very well (Ahluwalia and Mahmud, 2004). Yet UN agencies often neglect to apply such country-specific insights[47].

Combining lack of local knowledge with donor ideas that are currently 'in vogue' can lead to a project design that cannot be implemented or may even be counterproductive. According to the 'inclusion' agenda in the SWAp for primary education (PEDP-II), indigenous or tribal children are to be given education through the medium of their mother tongue (an internationally recognised best practice). However, there are about 30 tribal groups in Chittagong Hill Tracts, besides the Chakmas, who do not have a written language. Even those tribal groups that have their own scripts often prefer their children to be taught in Bengali, even though they would like their language and culture to be preserved.

Another donor-supported item in the 'inclusion' agenda of the PEDP-II is to promote the mainstreaming of school enrolment for children with disabilities or special needs, so that they are schooled with other children. However, ministry officials think that this is not a socially acceptable idea in Bangladesh, while there are also practical problems related to provision of infrastructure suitable for children with physical

Learning from Experience

disabilities and the extra demands on teaching[48]. Even the internationally accepted idea of 'best practice' in this respect has shifted back and forth. Yet another 'inclusion' agenda of the PEDP-II is to attract children from poor and vulnerable groups into school, with the exact mechanism for achieving this objective left to expatriate consultants (the project has provision for appointing such consultants).

The above examples seem to give at least some credence to common misgivings about the way aid agencies work. **Donors are often accused of offering what they want to give, not what the poor can use.** They design projects based on 'right ideas', without considering the country-specific institutional context. When no ready-made institutional arrangement is found for achieving the project goal, the task is left for expatriate consultants, as if such consultants can readily transplant solutions from abroad. In the case of the PEDP-II, ministry officials, in fact, had no illusion about what the expatriate consultants could achieve. Instead, they have taken their own initiatives to devise appropriate institutional arrangements to solve the above problems, by using the expertise of their own officials and locally hired consultants[49].

There are, however, examples of successful innovative ideas coming from donor agencies. The World Bank's recently launched project of community-driven local governance has already been mentioned. Another example is the ADB's Urban Primary Healthcare Project, which has built on the knowledge gathered from the ADB's long experience in working with the problems of the urban sector in Bangladesh. The project is based on a partnership between NGOs and local-government bodies (city corporations and municipalities) for improved delivery of primary health care, including reproductive health[50]. Under the project, service delivery is contracted out to NGOs through a bidding process; corporations/municipalities provide physical facilities, medicines and equipment, while the contracted NGOs provide services through recruitment of medical staff. There is both cost-recovery and special targeting of the poor. The project has been so successful that it is now being expanded to more municipalities, and the ADB has been joined by several other donors[51].

There are important lessons to be drawn from the experience of the above project. The project was initiated on the basis of an assessment that there was both need and capacity for such a project, and that there was strong support from the government. The original project design stipulated that the recruitment of NGOs would be through international bidding – a totally misguided policy for a country with such a strong presence of NGOs with experience in primary health-care delivery. Donor officials were subsequently persuaded to opt for local bidding. This crucial change in the original project design was possible only because of the proactive role of some staff members in the ADB's local office and headquarters, who were familiar with Bangladesh. As a result of this change, the cost of the project came down significantly – since contracting out to foreign NGOs would have involved high overhead costs for management. The project also made very little use of expatriate consultants. There were two expatriate consultants, both of whom performed poorly; indeed one was replaced by a local consultant, which was possible only because of the flexible attitude taken by the concerned ADB officials. According to current practice, replacing consultants financed by external resources is beyond the authority of government ministries or agencies[52].

Lessons can also be drawn from the experience of the SWAps in the health and primary education sectors, as mentioned above. The Health and Population Sector Programme (HPSP) was the first SWAp in Bangladesh – a World Bank-led multi-year programme (1998–2003), which was designed almost as a blueprint for the ICPD Programme of Action[53]. It aimed at integrating family planning and reproductive health and promoting rural health care by setting up an extensive network of community-driven rural health centres across the country. The programme looked perfect on paper, but was unworkable. It lacked ownership and was clearly over-designed in terms of resource needs and institutional arrangements, such as restructuring the entire health administration and mobilising community participation. Different donors promoted different issues, and exotic but mostly unworkable ideas were introduced by expatriate consultants[54]. By the end of the programme, thousands of newly constructed health centres remained unused, a domiciliary family planning service was withdrawn without its being replaced by integrated reproductive health care and both administrative re-structuring and community participation proved unworkable.

A new SWAp for the health sector, called HNPSP (the 'N' added for 'nutrition'), was launched to cover the period 2005–2010. It is claimed that there has been more local participation in its project design, but it still appears to lack effective ownership. There is provision for setting up a number of project-support units, which would be tanta-mount to running a parallel administration, bypassing the government systems. The system of centralised bulk procurement through international bidding has been found to be time consuming, and is burdensome for small local purchases. As in the case of the HPSP, the choice of appropriate project managers remains a problem due to the strong doctors' lobby.

The design of the other SWAp in primary education led by the ADB (the PEDP-II, being implemented during 2003–2009) looks more modest and locally owned. It uses the existing administrative set-up almost entirely, and has a much more sparing use of expatriate consultants (notwithstanding the problems discussed earlier). **Interestingly, the donors' own progress report comments that the programme design does not have a sufficiently large team of international experts to move from design to implementa-tion. Ministry officials do point to the extra burden of work involved in implementing the programme, but they in fact claim to have bargained successfully with donors to reduce international consultancy.** In contrast to the health sector's SWAp, procure-ment is decentralised and mostly local, although parallel government and donor proce-dures have to be followed. The programme has the government's strong support, along with a dedicated team of ministry officials that allows some governance problems to be avoided through 'ring-fencing' of its activities.

There are still some anomalies or ambiguities in the design of the PEDP-II. The milestone indicators for evaluation, for example, remain contentious. The intermediate indicators, like the increased number of trained teachers, the number of newly built classrooms or even the increase in enrolment, may not fully capture the attainment of the ultimate goal, namely, the quality of learning. That goal may be compromised by governance-related problems such as teacher absenteeism. This problem has recently surfaced in discussion on the effectiveness of the World Bank's worldwide lending operations in promoting basic education[55]. The PEDP-II proposes putting some funds at the disposal of the head teachers without providing for accountability. In terms of school construction work, however, ministry officials have devised on their own a simple mecha-nism for ensuring accountability: the public display of information regarding the con-struction work and permanent engraving of the name of the contractor and the date of construction.

The lessons learnt so far are that, in spite of the many potential advantages of a SWAp, undertaking such an approach is a challenging task, particularly for the lead donor. Given the multiplicity of donors with their respective policy agendas and the weaknesses of the implementing government agencies, efforts at co-ordination and harmonisation may prove difficult. Even in the case of the relatively modest PEDP-II, which really deals with a sub-sector (i.e. primary education), there are conflicts over reporting, disbursements and fiduciary requirements. Each donor seeks visibility for its own domestic reasons. There were 55 donor representatives in one mission, excluding local donor officials, with the government having to field an equally large negotiating team to match the strength of the donor mission. The individual donors brought their own consultants, even though the SWAp had been intended as a pooled arrangement. **The success of SWAps in Bangladesh in future will depend on more effective co-ordination among donors and avoiding the over-design of programmes.**

Even individual donor-funded projects may also sometimes be over-designed and too ambitious. **In contrast to homespun institutional arrangements, set up by insiders in response to concrete needs, these projects seek to introduce grand social engineering that seldom works.** The worldwide experience of such donor-driven projects is extensively discussed in a recent book by Easterly (2005). An example is the Danish aid agency, DANIDA's previous flagship project in Bangladesh known as the Noakhali Rural Development Project, implemented during 1978–1992. It was one of the largest projects implemented by DANIDA anywhere in the world, and was at that time considered an excellent example of integrated rural development – an approach that was in vogue in the 1970s and 1980s. An in-depth ex-post impact study of the project by DANIDA found that although the project had some beneficial effects on the region's economy, most of the goals, including sustainability, remained unfulfilled. **Among the weaknesses specifically cited by the study were too much reliance on expatriate advisers and a top-down set-up bypassing government systems**[56]. More than 60 long-term expatriate advisers – most of them Danish – worked two or three years each on the project.

There are other contemporary examples of donor-funded projects aimed at institutional innovations. With changes in ideas about aid, the focus of these projects has of course changed to such areas as SME development, supporting the livelihoods of the extreme poor and improving service delivery to the poor. Projects are certainly well-intentioned, but the key to success lies in finding sustainable ways of supporting home-grown ideas. Too many donors working in the same field can also create problems – if they are working at cross-purposes and in a way that neglects to reinforce the impact of one another. DFID's *Chars* Livelihoods Programme, for example, is an ambitious approach to help the extreme poor. DFID admittedly has a great deal of worldwide experience in such projects (DFID, 1999). It is, however, unclear if this programme is being co-ordinated with other such programmes and whether or not it relies excessively on expatriate consultancy[57]. **Experience in Bangladesh shows that donor organisations can design projects better if they can draw upon in-house expertise instead of hiring consultants, perhaps because of the difference in the 'reputation' incentives involved.**

The foregoing discussion should not be taken as making a case against technical assistance (TA). In fact, setting an arbitrary upper limit to the proportion of project expenditure to be spent on TA, as is practiced by the ERD, may be counterproductive. There are genuine needs for TA in Bangladesh in many areas, such as infrastructure development, product standardisation, technology transfer and export facilitation. Unfortunately, instead of being demand-driven, TA has been largely misused in the past.

It is understandable why donors often have to rely on expatriate consultants in their efforts to micro-manage projects. Even if this serves some immediate purpose in safe-guarding project implementation, it creates problems of sustainability by creating paral-lel structures. It is also most likely that the government agencies, which need technical support most, are also the ones who lack expertise in supervising the work of external consultants and demanding appropriate services from them. However, efforts to train local staff can be highly beneficial, and this aspect of TA needs careful consideration. In this respect, donors have genuine concerns about the deficiencies of the government's policies regarding training of officials, which render such training largely ineffective. **One of the main issues raised in the Aid Governance Initiative of 2003, mentioned earlier, was the effectiveness of foreign-assisted training.**

While there are areas where TA is genuinely needed, much it has been intended to support the kind of social engineering that can hardly be achieved without local ideas and input. At times, TA has been offered even to help the institutional development of micro-credit in Bangladesh (which is like carrying coal to Newcastle or even worse). **It may be noted, however, that the World Bank's large credit programmes for supporting the PKSF – Bangladesh's highly reputed organisation, which funds the micro-credit operations of NGOs – have never had any provision for expatriate consultants. It is worth studying whether the aid industry built around TA has something to do with the white-collar job market and the employability of the potential consultants in their home countries**[58].

V   Concluding remarks

The preceding chapter has attempted to contribute to the development debate in Bangladesh by highlighting various aspects of recent aid experience relevant to the Poverty Reduction Strategy process. It advances certain propositions regarding existing aid modalities by way of citing some rather randomly selected examples and cannot, therefore, claim to provide any comprehensive account of the issues covered. It is also admittedly 'a snapshot of a moving target' – to quote from the comments by a donor official[59] – since these aid modalities have been undergoing significant changes in recent years.

Since the mid-1980s, Bangladesh has embarked on wide-ranging market-oriented policy reforms under fairly rigid aid conditionality[60]. Changing to a new mode of aid relationships based on policy ownership, result orientation and mutual accountability will not be easy. Above all, it will require a change in the mindsets of both donors and the government. For example, until recently, one of the major donor concerns was how to provide **additional** funds to (donors') priority areas, since the government might di-vert its own funds to lower-priority areas in response to the availability of foreign funds – the so-called problem of **aid fungibility**[61]. According to the PRSP process, the concern is now apparently the other way around – that is, whether donor support is sufficiently aligned to the country-owned public spending priorities. **Even if the aid conditionalities now reappear in other forms, this represents a significant change at least in the outward form and format of donor engagement.**

The true worth of the proposed new rules of engagement will be tested by how far the PRSP can go beyond the donor-driven agenda, and whether the PRSP is seen in Bangladesh as a vehicle for mobilising foreign assistance or if it genuinely represents an overall national-development strategy. These are also questions related to the 'ownership' of the PRSP process. The aid dependence of Bangladesh has been declining fairly rapidly over the last two decades – with the ratio of gross foreign aid to GDP declining from around 8 per cent in the late 1980s to the recent level of about 2 per cent. **The PRS process has thus been initiated at a time when committing to a national development agenda does not make sense if the purpose is to satisfy donor concerns alone[62]. As the leverage of aid conditionality weakens, donors also need to look for other modalities of engagement. Viewed in this way, there are incentives on both sides for making the PRS process an effective one.**

Moreover, Bangladesh has already gone through the initial phases of economic liberalisation and market-oriented reforms; the reform process has now entered a stage of 'learning-by-doing', where looking at the actual outcomes is at least as important for policy-makers as understanding the *ex ante* rationale for reform. It is no coincidence that donors are increasingly concerned about finding a 'local fit' for their projects and programmes, while at the same time taking advantage of their global experience[63]. This calls for moving from predetermined aid conditionality to result-orientation – a move that is in line with the PRS process. It also calls for donors to be more accountable and to be able to benefit from lessons learnt from past experience[64].

Donors are also taking steps towards aid harmonisation. The effectiveness of such initiatives needs to be judged in the light of their actual contribution to reducing aid delivery costs or increasing aid effectiveness. It is well known that donors do not always speak with one voice and they have different agendas to pursue. A single framework of conditions in a multi-donor approach can even be counterproductive, by reducing flexibility in pursuing various development ideas and resulting in too many conditions. **The success of aid harmonisation efforts thus depends to a large extent on donors' genuine commitment, along with finding trustworthy partners within government.**

There is no easy answer regarding how to provide aid in a governance-challenged environment, such as that that exists in Bangladesh. It should be noted, however, that in spite of governance-related constraints, Bangladesh has achieved notable success in accelerating GDP growth and reducing poverty[65]. Even more impressive have been the improvements in social and human development indicators, particularly in respect of infant and child mortality, female school enrolment and the adoption of birth control. It remains a puzzle how Bangladesh could make such remarkable progress in social development, despite widespread poverty and poor governance in public service delivery. The early gains from the adoption of easy low-cost solutions, the contribution of NGOs towards raising public awareness, favourable budgetary allocations and donor support have all helped[66]. However, sustaining these positive trends in poverty reduction and human development may become increasingly difficult without larger social spending and a further acceleration in GDP growth. It should also to be noted that the gross aid received by Bangladesh is much lower compared to the average of low-income countries, both as a proportion of GDP and in per capita terms; and this disparity has been increasing over the years[67]. It thus poses a challenge to the donor community to find ways of helping Bangladesh to achieve its development goals.

Notes

1. This report was prepared by Professor Wahiduddin Mahmud in August 2006. Dr Bishakha Mukherjee was the Commonwealth Secretariat consultant on this project.
2. The draft I-PRSP was posted on the government's website in April 2002.
3. For example, DANIDA, the Danish aid agency, reportedly delayed the preparation of its aid programme document, Bangladesh-Denmark Partnership: Strategy for Development Cooperation 2005-2009, until the final PRSP was made available (Ministry of Foreign Affairs of Denmark, 2005).
4. Cf. The Report of the Panel of Economists on the Draft Fifth Five Year Plan, General Economics Division, Planning Commission, 1997; reproduced in Mahmud (2002), ch.20.
5. Centre for Policy Dialogue (CPD), 1995.
6. The government did indeed approach the UNDP for assistance in the preparation of the I-PRSP, but eventually preferred not to accept the UNDP's offer of using the services of one of its staff members based in New York.
7. The thematic groups were in turn provided with consultancy services by researchers from the Bangladesh Institute of Development Studies (BIDS).
8. The outcome of the exercise was several district-wise plan documents, as well as a national document called the Participatory Perspective Plan 1995-2010 (Government of Bangladesh, 1995).
9. For the results of this exercise, see Bhattacharya and Titumir (2001); also see Mahmud (2002), ch.1.
10. During the 1990s, the average annual growth of per capita income accelerated to above 3 per cent compared to the 1.6 per cent of the earlier decade, while the poverty incidence by headcount estimate declined by about 1 percentage point a year. However, more recent poverty estimates available since the preparation of the PRSP show that the poverty incidence declined by almost 2 percentage points a year between 2000 and 2005.
11. For a discussion on this, see Ahmed and Mahmud (2006), ch.2, pp.40-43.
12. This item is specially mentioned in the policy agenda for Roads and Highways, besides being included under the policy matrix for governance.
13. World Bank (2006) *Bangladesh Country Assistance Strategy 2006-2009*, p.63.
14. See chapter VIII of the final PRSP, Government of Bangladesh (2005).
15. See Osmani (2006); World Bank (2003), p.55.
16. Cf. the final PRSP document, Government of Bangladesh (2005), p.187.
17. For a detailed discussion of the political economy of public development spending in Bangladesh, see Mahmud (2002).
18. Cf. Government of Bangladesh (2006), pp.2-5.
19. This committee will have representation from the Implementation, Monitoring and Evaluation Division (IMED) of the Planning Ministry, which is the agency responsible for the regular monitoring of the implementation of development projects.
20. Despite recent progress, for example, the World Bank's country portfolio continues to have a large undisbursed amount, totalling $1.5 billion at the end of FY05. This implies a disbursement ratio of 23 per cent. The disbursement ratio of ADB's aid to Bangladesh is even lower – about 13 per cent at the end of the calendar year of 2005; this is because the ADB's assistance is largely provided as project lending rather than budgetary support. (The disbursement ratio shows the ratio of disbursements during the fiscal year to the undisbursed balance at the beginning of the fiscal year).
21. This initiative followed the global trend for aid harmonisation as laid down in the Rome Declaration 2003, and the recommendations arising out of it were made available for the Bangladesh Development Forum Meeting held in May 2003.

22. For example, the Canadian aid agency (CIDA) does not apply its procurement rule if procurement is from a Canadian company.
23. However, it should be noted that over 80 per cent of PEDP-II expenditures follow the government's local procedures.
24. This excludes the DFID missions, which are conducted by the local office.
25. This is mainly required to meet the respective aid agencies' internal requirements on form and format.
26. The 'joint strategy outcomes by partners' is a continuing exercise in which donors other than the big four are also invited to join.
27. The common policy agenda includes such actions as establishing a private seaport, introduction of e-governance for procurement and rationalisation of agricultural subsidies.
28. Such an indicator may be supplemented by information on the quality of service.
29. The outcomes matrix of the joint CAS does show the specific projects of the four donor partners that relate to the broad strategies.
30. This is based on the actual utilisation of aid and the actual spending under the Annual Development Plan, as estimated by the Implementation, Monitoring and Evaluation Division (IMED) of the Planning Ministry.
31. According to a top Bangladesh government official, 'there is little incentive within the government to prepare aid-worthy projects, because the officials are used to spoon-feeding by the donors'.
32. The Australian aid agency was recently interested in providing funds in certain development areas, but did not know what to do as the ministries allegedly could not help it to prioritise the use of funds.
33. See, for example, the World Bank's joint CAS (World Bank, 2006, p.63). This is true also in the case of the donors other than the 'big four'. The Swiss SDC, for example, uses the CPD, a local thin-tank, as a platform for consultations. The results of local consultations were included in an in-depth evaluation of the Netherlands' development programme in Bangladesh; see Netherlands Ministry of Foreign Affairs (1998), Reports 1, 2 and 3.
34. Interestingly, only 2 per cent of aid cancellations had been due to misprocurement, as reported in an unpublished annex to the World Bank's 2006 CAS document. For a discussion on the quality of the Bank's portfolio performance in Bangladesh, see World Bank (2006), p.69.
35. The project called the Local Government Support Project will be funded by an IDA credit of about US$100 million.
36. PROSPER stands for 'promoting financial services for poverty reduction in Bangladesh'; this is a multi-donor project involving US$73 million in grants.
37. South Asia Enterprise Development Facility.
38. In this respect, local donor officials admit that Bangladesh's repeated ranking as the most corrupt country by Transparency International has had an adverse impact.
39. Even then, Bangladesh remains one of the largest recipients of IDA loans; in FY03, for example, it was in fact the largest IDA-only recipient and second overall after India.
40. This refers to FY05; see World Bank (2006), p.68, table 6.
41. The assessment was undertaken by the World Bank's Quality Assurance Group (QAG).
42. While previous attempts to reduce the very high rates of electricity pilferage failed to produce results, the recent performance of the Dhaka Electricity Supply Corporation (DESCO) appears promising.
43. Palli Karma-Sahayak Foundation, Local Government Engineering Department and Rural Electrification Board.
44. This example has been mentioned in the PRSP document. See also Rahman (2006), p.15.
45. Rahman, (2006), p.16.

46. This, however, remains a contentious issue between local experts and UN officials; see the UNFPA response to the draft version of this chapter and comments by Dr Zafrullah Chowdhury of Gono Shasthya Kendra (GK) at www.ergonline.org [accessed 5 September 2008].

47. According to the results of the Bangladesh Demographic and Health Survey 2004, 63 per cent of women do not know about the benefits of antenatal care and another 13 per cent are not aware of the existence of the service. One successful, home-grown programme for reducing maternal mortality is that of the Ganashasthya Kendra (GK) – Bangladesh's world-renowned health care NGO. The programme uses the services of trained TBAs, along with referrals to the public-health facilities.

48. Under same-school enrolment, children with disabilities are found frequently to drop out because of teasing and bullying.

49. Ministry officials are considering, for example, the idea of school meals to attract children from poor communities and setting up of boarding schools in the Hill Tracts region, where the remoteness of settlements is the main constraint to schooling.

50. The SWAp in the health sector does not cover urban areas.

51. The project started as a pilot for 2000–2005, and at the time of writing had entered the second expanded phase.

52. See World Bank (2006), p.82, endnote 3.

53. The so-called Cairo Declaration of the International Conference on Population and Development held in 1994.

54. Some academics, however, saw this as a merit of the project; see, for example, Jahan (2003).

55. See Banerjee, Cole, Duflo and Linden (2005).

56. See Ministry of Foreign Affairs, DANIDA (2002); pp.33–34.

57. The programme has allegedly a very large technical assistance component.

58. Griffin (1996, pp.11–13) discusses how developing countries have received technical assistance that they neither want nor need.

59. See the comments by David Wood, country representative of DFID in Bangladesh (www.ergonline.org [accessed 5 September 2008]).

60. Mahmud (2001), ch.3.

61. In fact, one of the stated rationales for introducing the sector-wide approach in the health sector (the HPSP 1998–2003) was to ensure that an appropriate proportion of total public health spending would go to primary health care.

62. In this view, assessing progress in aid effectiveness commitments may be seen as being only a part of monitoring the implementation of the overall development strategy.

63. As part of this effort, some donors report that they are increasingly relying on local expertise in designing their projects and programmes: see the comments by Hua Du, country director at the Bangladesh Resident Mission of the ADB (www.ergonline.org [accessed 5 September 2008]).

64. According to a donor official, the seminar to discuss the draft version of the report upon which this chapter is based was itself an example of a 'local mechanism' for ensuring joint donor-country accountability; see the comments by Christine I Wallich, country director of the World Bank (www.ergonline.org [accessed 5 September 2008]).

65. Ibid.

66. On this, see Ahluwalia and Mahmud (2004) and Mahmud (2003).

67. According to the World Bank's World Development Indicators, gross aid as a per cent of GNP in Bangladesh was 2.8 per cent in 1998 compared to the average of 4.7 per cent for all low-income countries excluding China and India; in 1993, the figures were 4 per cent and 5.2 per cent respectively.

Annex

Summary of 2002 report of the Independent Monitoring Group (IMG): enhancing aid relationships in Tanzania

1.0 Background and context

The 2003 Independent Monitoring Group (IMG) report was an outcome of a substantial history of reviews, which have examined the relationships between the Government of Tanzania (GoT) and aid donors conducted by observers independent of both sides. Relations between the two sides deteriorated to a low level in the early 1990s. In order to address this situation, an independent group of experts led by Professor Gerald K Helleiner was appointed to study the situation and make recommendations. The study was completed in 1995 and subsequent discussions between government and donors were based on that report. Based on the Helleiner report and following a change of government, concerted efforts involving dialogue between the government and donors were initiated in 1996. This was followed by an agreement in January 1997 between the GoT and its development partners to jointly set out a programme to redefine the terms of their development co-operation. The result was a set of 'agreed notes' (in the form of 18 points) stating, among other things, that there was a need to ensure enhanced government leadership in development programming, increased transparency, accountability and efficiency in aid delivery. The elaboration of a framework for co-operation culminated in the preparation of the Tanzania Assistance Strategy (TAS) from 1998/99, finally published in 2002. TAS is meant to be a framework for partnership that would also define the role of external resources for development.

2.0 Methodology

The group was chaired by Professor Samuel Wangwe and its work was undertaken during the course of 2002, under the administrative auspices of the Economic and Social Research Foundation (ESRF), Dar es Salaam. The group as a whole met twice, in March and June 2002, but locally based members undertook further work between those dates and thereafter. The IMG made use of relevant background materials, both as related to Tanzania and the wider literature, but the bulk of the analysis was based on a large number of interviews with officials of departments of government and all official donors with substantial aid programmes in the country, bilateral and multilateral.

3.0 Benchmarks

It is perhaps useful to assess the situation as the group found it in 2002 against two benchmarks: (a) the situation as described in the 1995 Helleiner report; and (b) as described more recently in his 1999 and 2000 reports. By either comparison, but especially the first, the group concluded that major improvements have occurred: indeed the state of GoT-donor relations is matched in only a few other aid-dependent states of Africa.

4.0 Main findings

4.1 Considerable progress had been made

The report describes the various ways in which progress had been made:
(i)   improved channels of dialogue;
(ii)   the trend away from project aid;
(iii) the development of sector-wide approaches;
(iv)   technical assistance has been changing;
(v)   procurement tying is on the decline;
(vi)   reporting of aid flows is improving; and
(vii) Consultative Group Meetings had become more participative.

The basic message was that GOT-donor relations had improved. By comparison with 1995 and since the Helleiner report of 2000, donor-GoT relations were much improved. Donors had greater trust in the government and they had responded in various ways to improve their own policies and practices.

Two general points emerged. The first was the powerful influence of the trend towards programme aid. That is not only desirable in itself, as likely to raise aid effectiveness and lower associated transactions costs, but it had also fed into a number of the other improvements recorded in the report. The second point was that there are marked differences in the extent to which individual donors had been willing and able to respond to the felt deficiencies in past aid delivery systems and to improvements on the side of the GoT. This pointed to an opportunity for making overall improvement through peer pressure, a situation which is likely to bear fruit the more the government continues to assert its leadership in aid co-ordination.

4.2 The basis for the improvements achieved

Both the GoT and donors had responded to improve on the dire situation of the mid-1990s.

4.2.1 On the government side:
(i)   The emergence of a demonstrated commitment to improvement of relations with donors had been fundamental. This had been demonstrated in terms of the trend towards increased openness, transparency and accountability in the conduct of government business, and specifically to the administration of the budget.
(ii)   The Poverty Reduction Strategy (PRS) and the respective participatory working groups signified improvement in policy formation with greater focus and prioritisation. Subsequently, the Poverty Monitoring System (PMS) and Participatory Poverty Assessment (PPA) were put in place to monitor and assess developments in poverty in a more transparent and participatory manner.
(iii) The development of the public expenditure review/medium-term expenditure framework (PER/MTEF) into an important instrument for a more transparent,

goal-oriented and integrated budgetary process. The creation of the Tanzania Revenue Authority was also an important move.

(iv) The computer-based Integrated Financial Management System, designed to raise the efficiency and integrity of public finance management, had also contributed to increased donor confidence and to the observed trend towards a progressive switch from project to programme aid modalities.

(v) The publication and launching in 2002 of the government's TAS. The significance of the TAS is in the potential it has for further developing Tanzanian ownership of the activities supported by its development partners and for steering aid provisions to meet local needs.

(vi) Increased openness, transparency and commitment to dialogue in the conduct of government business was reported in many of the IMG interviews.

(vii) A greater degree of Tanzanian 'ownership' of policies and processes by comparison with the bleak situation in the mid-1990s.

(viii) The emergence of a political leadership committed to the rebuilding of constructive relationships with donor partners.

4.2.2 On the donor side:

(i) Donors had been willing to revisit their own experiences, to be self-critical and to accept independent assessment.

(ii) Donors had learned from past experience and had to a large extent accepted that some of their policies have not been effective in the past.

(iii) Many donors had shown willingness to adapt and respond flexibly to improvements made and initiatives taken by GoT. Not all donors had been able to move at the same pace, but the direction of change was appreciable on the part of most.

(iv) The highly constructive and fruitful role of the local Development Assistance Committee (DAC) had contributed in an important measure to the unusually good degree of donor harmonisation and co-ordination observed by the IMG. The local DAC appeared to be able to combine an inclusive approach in the face of widely varying agency views and policies with the exertion of a positive peer pressure on what the group called the laggard or unpersuaded agencies.

(v) The changed outlook of the World Bank was notable, especially when seen in the context of the 1995 Helleiner report, which had singled out the World Bank as being unwilling to listen and arrogant, as placing little real weight on local ownership and as relying excessively on conditionality. The IMG found that the Bank had come to play a highly constructive role, supportive of many positive developments identified in the report.

(vi) A reduced reliance on policy conditionality. Co-ordinated and partnership-based approaches were increasingly replacing one-sided conditionalities.

(vii) Donors' stated desire to reduce the transactions costs to government of utilising the aid offered to it. This desire had been demonstrated through initiatives to improve co-ordination.

(viii) The change in the venue for meetings of the Consultative Group to Dar es Salaam, and its opening up to a wider range of stakeholders.

Donors had therefore contributed importantly to improving aid relationships in Tanzania. To some extent, the donor changes just described reflect general shifts of donor thinking on aid effectiveness. What impressed the IMG, however, is that, in many respects, these changes had gone further in Tanzania than in most countries. The growing element of trust and the acceptance of independent assessment and monitoring had contributed to these outcomes. The case of Tanzania could therefore offer some useful lessons to other countries.

5.0 Areas for further improvement

Nonetheless, the IMG saw many areas where further progress was needed. Although most of the suggestions presented applied to both GoT and development partners, some proposals applied primarily to GoT and others to the donors.

5.1 Government side

Suggestions were made in respect of five areas:
  (i)   strengthening dialogue by increasing openness and improving channels of dia-
        logue and encouraging more sectors to adopt sector-wide approaches (SWAps);
  (ii) encouraging moves towards programme aid by consolidating current PER/MTEF
        processes, public financial accountability and anti-corruption measures;
  (iii) addressing capacity constraints by undertaking a national capacity needs assess-
        ment of priority areas of intervention, accelerating the implementation of the
        PSRP (especially the pay reform) and decentralisation;
  (iv) addressing aid dependence by making the exit strategy a more explicit policy
        objective with time-bound targets; and
  (v)   strengthening Tanzanian ownership by being more explicit in setting priorities,
        being more assertive about preferred forms of aid and being more willing to say
        'no' to non-priority or distortive offers.

5.2 Donor side

On the side of the donors, suggestions were made in seven areas:
  (i)   further improving the composition of aid by continuing the trend towards more
        programme aid, exerting peer pressure under government leadership;
  (ii) learning lessons from SWAps by continuing to lower transaction costs and
        promoting local ownership, while striving to harmonise procurement and re-
        porting procedures. Donors should support GoT's efforts in improving policy
        analysis and implementation capacities and focusing more on wider challenges
        of delivering results and monitoring performance. Donors and GoT should
        accord priority to institutionalisation of SWAps by promoting their replication
        to other sectors, enhancing participation and co-ordination and integrating
        them more effectively into the PER/MTEF processes;
  (iii) reducing the vulnerability of programme aid to political uncertainty by develop-
        ing safeguards (in the form of an agreed code of good practice) against sudden
        withdrawal of promised levels of programme support;
  (iv) raising the effectiveness of technical assistance (TA) by taking action in three
        areas: first, accepting the principle of using TA primarily for local capacity
        building; second, drawing lessons from existing practices of TA pooling with a

view to building on positive experiences; and third, facilitating the GoT to take the lead in formulating programmes for local capacity building, to which TA can contribute;

(v) further improving donor co-ordination by incorporating in the TAS agreements on common reporting and joint missions, establishing 'quiet times', adopting selectivity to avoid competitive overcrowding in some sectors, while other priority sectors are under-supported, and continuing to integrate donor-support initiatives in the PRS;

(vi) empowering agencies to play a full partnership role by consolidating initiatives being taken towards greater agency decentralisation and equipping them to enhance their capacity to make decisions; and

(vii) rationalising the fora for dialogue with a view to reducing overlap and achieving greater integration into PER/MTEF processes and the PRS.

6.0 Further monitoring arrangements

The experience in the 2002 IMG evaluation also suggested some ideas for future monitoring arrangements. In this regard, suggestions were made in four areas:

(i) undertaking periodic stock-taking in more specific areas as identified by the joint GoT/DAC machinery for implementing the TAS;

(ii) GoT and donor performance monitoring as two sides of the coin: the monitoring of performance should apply to both sides;

(iii) performance indicators to be largely qualitative, but further quantitative indicators can play a supplementary role. Performance indicators should continue to be developed in the Joint TAS Implementation machinery; and

(iv) replicating the Tanzania experience in other aid-dependent countries.

References

Tanzania

Chapman, Erin, eDATA (2004) Meeting the Millennium Challenge. Debt, Aid and Trade for Africa.

Development Assistance Committee (2003) Peer Review, Tanzania. Paris: Organisation for Economic Co-operation and Development.

Development Partners Group (2003) Architecture Task Force Briefing Note. Tanzania: DPG.

Evans, A and E Ngalwea (2001) 'Institutionalizing the PRSP approach in Tanzania'. Chapter 9 in PRSP Institutionalization Study: Final Report. Overseas Development Institute (ODI) and Research on Poverty Alleviation (REPOA), submitted to the Strategic Partnership with Africa. London: ODI.

Government of Tanzania (2000) Poverty Reduction Strategy Paper. Dar es Salaam: Government of Tanzania.

Government of Tanzania (2001) Poverty Reduction Strategy Paper, Progress Report 2000/01. Dar es Salaam: Government of Tanzania.

Government of Tanzania (2003) Poverty Reduction Strategy Paper, Progress Report 2001/02. Dar es Salaam: Government of Tanzania.

Government of Tanzania (2003a) Action Plan for the Implementation of the Tanzania Assistance Strategy. Dar es Salaam: Government of Tanzania.

Government of Tanzania (2003b) Tanzania Assistance Strategy – Annual Implementation Report FY2002/03. Dar es Salaam: Government of Tanzania.

Government of Tanzania, Vice-President's Office (2003) Guide for Poverty Reduction Strategy Review. Dar es Salaam: Government of Tanzania.

Government of Tanzania, Ministry of Finance (2004) Public Expenditure Review: Medium Term Expenditure Framework (MTEF) Cross Sector Strategy. Dar es Salaam: Government of Tanzania.

GTZ (2003) Parliaments in sub-Saharan Africa: Actors in Poverty Reduction. Eschborn: Deutsche Gesellschaft für Technische Zusammenarbeit (GTZ).

IMF (2003) Tanzania: Sixth review under the PRGF and related documents. Washington, DC: International Monetary Fund.

IMF (2004) Tanzania: First review under the three year PRGF and related documents. Washington, DC: International Monetary Fund.

Independent Monitoring Group (2002) Enhancing Aid Relationships in Tanzania: Report of the Independent Monitoring Group. Dar es Salaam: Economic and Social Research Foundation.

KK Consulting Associates (2001) Tanzania: Poverty Reduction Strategy Paper – An Assessment of the Depth of Understanding of the PRSP in the Government. Nairobi, Kenya: KK Consulting Associates.

Mwakasege, Christopher (2002) Making PRSPs work in a Globalised Economy. The Tanzanian Experience of Implementing PRSP for the First Two Years: an NGO perspective. Arusha: Tanzania Social and Economic Trust.

NGO Policy Forum (2004) Preliminary Submission for the Poverty Reduction Strategy Review. Dar es Salaam: NPF.

Operations Evaluation Department, World Bank, and Independent Evaluation Office, IMF (2004) Republic of Tanzania: Evaluation of Poverty Reduction Strategy Paper (PRSP) Process and

Arrangements under the Poverty Reduction and Growth Facility (PRGF). Washington, DC: World Bank and IMF.

Ronsholt, Frans (2002) OECD-DAC Study on Donor Burdens and Donor Good Practices, Tanzania Case Study. Paris: Organisation for Economic Co-operation and Development-Development Assistance Committee.

SPA-6 Budget Support Working Group (2004) Survey of the Alignment of Budget Support and Balance of Payments Support with National PRS Processes. BSWG.

Wangwe, Samuel (2001), Poverty Reduction Strategy Paper: Experiences and Lessons from Tanzania. Dar es Salaam: Economic and Social Research Foundation (ESRF).

World Bank (2004) Tanzania Public Expenditure Review FY04. Review of Fiscal Developments and Budget Management Issues FY03–FY 04: Joint Evaluation Report. Washington, DC: World Bank.

Ghana

Aryeetey, E and A McKay (2004) Operationalizing Pro-Poor Growth in Ghana, Mimeo. Legon: University of Ghana, Institute of Statistical, Social and Economic Research.

Booth, David, Richard Crook, E Gyimah-Boadi, Tony Killick and Robin Luckham, with Nana Boateng (2004) Drivers of Change in Ghana: Overview Report, Final Draft, 25 May 2004. London: Overseas Development Institute and Accra: Center for Democratic Development (CDD).

Coulombe, H and A McKay (2004) Selective poverty reduction in a slow growth environment: Ghana in the 1990s. Paper presented at the conference on Ghana's Economy at the Half Century, Accra 18–20 July 2004.

ISSER (2005) Socio-Economic Development in Ghana, Mimeo. Legon: University of Ghana, Institute of Statistical, Social and Economic Research.

Killick, T (2004) What Drives Change in Ghana? A Political-Economy View of Economic Prospects, Mimeo. Legon: University of Ghana, Institute of Statistical, Social and Economic Research.

Killick, T and C Abugre (2001) 'Institutionalising the PRSP Approach in Ghana'. In PRSP Institutionalisation Study: Final Report. London: ODI.

Wetzel, Deborah (2000) 'Promises and Pitfalls in Public Expenditure'. In Ernest Ayreety, Jane Harrigan and Machiko Nissanke (eds.) Economic Reforms in Ghana: the Miracle and the Mirage. Oxford: James Carrey and Accra: Woeli Publishing Services.

Malawi

Botolo, B (undated) 'Assessment of Poverty Reduction Strategy in Africa: The Case of Malawi'.

Chirwa, EW (2005) 'Poverty Reduction Strategies in Malawi: Processes, Implementation and Sustainability'. In Proceedings of the Workshop on Assessment of Poverty Reduction Strategy Papers in Sub-Saharan Africa: The Case of Malawi, held on 4 November 2005 in Lilongwe, Malawi.

Jenkins, R and M Tsoka (2003) 'Malawi'. Development Policy Review, Vol.21, No.2, pp.197–215.

Government of Malawi (2002) Poverty Reduction Strategy Paper. Lilongwe: Government of Malawi.

Tsoka, MG (2004) Assessment of the PRSPs: Can the Malawi PRSP reduce poverty this time around? Mimeo. Zomba: University of Malawi, Centre for Social Research.

Bangladesh

Ahluwalia, Isher J and W Mahmud (2004) 'Economic transformation and social development in Bangladesh'. *Economic and Political Weekly* (Mumbai), September 4-10 2004, Vol.XXXIX, No.36.

Ahmed, S and W Mahmud (eds.) (1996) *Growth and Poverty: The Development Experience in Bangladesh*. Dhaka: University Press Ltd and Washington, DC: World Bank.

Asian Development Bank (2005) Country *Strategy and Program 2006-2010: Bangladesh*. Manila: ADB (see: www.adb.org/Documents/CSPs [accessed 5 September 2008]).

Banarjee, Abhijit, Shawn Cole, Esther Duflo and Leigh Linden (2005) 'Remedying education'. National Bureau of Economic Research Working Paper 11904, December.

Bangladesh Bank (2006) *Financial Sector Review* (Dhaka), Vol.1, No.1, May 2006.

Bhattacharya, Debapriya and RAM Titumir (eds.) (2001) *Stakeholders' Perceptions: Reforms and Consequences*. Dhaka: Shraban Prakashani for SAPRI (Structural Adjustment Participatory Review Initiative).

DFID (1999) The livelihoods framework: sustainable livelihoods guidance sheets. London: Department for International Development.

Easterly, W (2006) *The White Man's Burden: Why the West's Efforts to Aid the Rest Have Done So Much Ill and So Little Good*. New York: Penguin Press.

Government of Bangladesh (2003) *Bangladesh: A National Strategy for Growth, Poverty Reduction and Social Development*. Dhaka: Economic Relations Division, Ministry of Finance, Government of Bangladesh.

Government of Bangladesh (2005) *Unlocking the Potential: National Strategy for Accelerated Poverty Reduction*. Dhaka: Planning Commission, General Economics Division, Government of Bangladesh.

Government of Bangladesh (2005a) *Flow of External Resources into Bangladesh*. Dhaka: Economic Relations Division, Ministry of Finance, Government of Bangladesh.

Government of Bangladesh (2006) *Medium Term Budgetary Framework*. Dhaka: Ministry of Finance, Government of Bangladesh.

Government of Bangladesh and United Nations (2005) *United Nations Development Assistance Framework in Bangladesh*. Dhaka: Office of the United Nations Resident Coordinator.

Government of Denmark, Ministry of Foreign Affairs, DANIDA (2002) Evaluation in the wake of a flagship: ex-post impact study of the Noakhali Rural Development Project in Bangladesh, Main report. Copenhagen: Centre for Development Research.

Government of Denmark, Ministry of Foreign Affairs, DANIDA (2005) *Bangladesh-Denmark Partnership: Strategy for Development Cooperation 2005-2009*. Copenhagen: Government of Denmark.

Government of the Netherlands, Ministry of Foreign Affairs (1998) Bangladesh: Evaluation of the Netherlands' Development Programme with Bangladesh, 1972-1996, Reports 1, 2 and 3. The Hague: Policy and Operations Evaluation Department, Ministry of Foreign Affairs.

Griffin, K and T McKinley (1996) 'New approaches to development cooperation'. Discussion Paper Series 7. New York: Office of Development Studies, United Nations Development Programme.

Jahan, Rounaq ((2003) 'Restructuring the health system: experiences of advocates for gender equity in Bangladesh'. *Reproductive Health Matters*, 11(21): pp.183-191 (see: www.rhm-elsevier.com [accessed 5 September 2008]).

Mahmud, W (2001) *Adjustment and Beyond: The Reform Experience in South Asia*. Palgrave-Macmillan in association with International Economic Association.

Mahmud, W (2002) *Popular Economics: Unpopular Essays*. Dhaka: University Press Ltd.

Mahmud, W (2002a) 'National budgets, social spending and public choice'. Working Paper No.162. Brighton: Institute for Development Studies (IDS) at the University of Sussex.

Mahmud, W (2003) 'Bangladesh: development outcomes and challenges in the context of global-ization'. Paper presented in the conference on The Future of Globalization: Explorations in the Light of Recent Turbulence, Yale Center for the Study of Globalization, 10–11 October 2003 (available at: www.ycsg.yale.edu [accessed 5 September 2008]).

Mahmud, W and S Mahmud (2000) Chapter 2: 'Bangladesh', in S Forman and R Ghosh, *Promoting Reproductive Health: Investing in Health for Development*. Boulder and London: Lynne Rienner Publishers for the Center for International Cooperation at New York University.

Osmani, SR (2006) 'Delivering basic health services in Bangladesh: a view from the human rights perspective'. In S Ahmed and W Mahmud (eds.) *Growth and Poverty: The Development Experience in Bangladesh*. Dhaka: University Press Ltd, and Washington, DC: World Bank.

Osmani, SR, W Mahmud, B Sen, H Dagdeviren and A Seth (2003) Macroeconomics of poverty reduction: the case of Bangladesh. Dhaka and Kathmandu: UNDP.

Rahman, Hossain Zillur (2006) Bangladesh 2015: crossing miles... PPRC Policy Paper. Dhaka: Power and Participation Research Centre.

World Bank (2003) *Poverty in Bangladesh: Building on Progress*. Document of the World Bank and Asian Development Bank. Washington, DC: World Bank.

World Bank (2003a) *Bangladesh: Public Expenditure Review*. Document of the World Bank and the Asian Development Bank. Washington, DC: World Bank.

World Bank (2003b) Bangladesh: Joint Staff Assessment of the interim Poverty Reduction Strategy Paper. Prepared by the staffs of the IDA and the IMF, Report No. 25888-BD. Washington, DC: World Bank.

World Bank (2005) Bangladesh: joint staff advisory note on the poverty reduction strategy paper. Prepared by the staffs of the IDA and the IMF, Report No. 34448-BD. World Bank: Washington, DC.

World Bank (2006) Bangladesh Country Assistance Strategy 2006–2009. Prepared jointly by ADB, DFID and Japan. Washington, DC: World Bank (www.worldbank.org.bd [accessed 5 September 2008]).

Index

accountability 4–5
   Bangladesh 109
   GPRS 47, 60
   Tanzania 18–19
ADB *see* Asian Development Bank
ADP *see* Annual Development Plan
Aid Governance Initiative, Bangladesh 101
Annual Development Plan (ADP),
   Bangladesh 98, 103
annual progress reports (APRs)
   GPRS 39–42, 50, 59
   MPRSP 70–1
Aryeetey, Ernest 33–63
Asian Development Bank (ADB) 91, 101–2,
   104, 107, 109, 111

Bangladesh Harmonisation Action Plan 101
Bangladesh and PRS/PRSP 1–2, 91–115
   consensus on agenda 94–7
   donor support 100–6
   government initiative 97–106
   implementation 97–106
   improving aid provision 106–9
   local knowledge 110–14
   monitoring 97–100
   outcomes of PRS 102–3
   quality of strategy 92–7
   technical assistance 110–14
Bangladesh Water Development Board 99
basket funding 12, 23
bottom up strategies 20
Bretton Woods Institutions (BWIs) 12–13,
   18–19, 29, 65
   see also International Monetary Fund;
   World Bank
budgets
   Bangladesh 95, 98–9
   GPRS
      annual progress reports 40
      development partner support 54
      implementation of PRS 49–50
      MDBS 53, 55–7, 61–2
   MPRSP
      CABS 82–3
      development partner support 88

      implementing PRS 79–80
      integration into systems 69–70
      lessons learnt 90
   Tanzania
      annual process 12
      development partners 23–5
      donor timing 25–6
      improving support modalities 30–1
      integrating donor funds 14
      lessons learnt 32
BWIs *see* Bretton Woods Institutions

CABS *see* Common Approach to Budget
   Support
CAS *see* country-assistance strategies
Chipeta, Chinyamata 65–90
civil society 3–4
   Bangladesh 104–5
   Malawi 76, 86
   Tanzania 17–18
Co-ordinated Programme for Economic and
   Social Development (CPESD), Ghana
   37–8, 58
Common Approach to Budget Support
   (CABS), Malawi 82–3
communication of strategy, MPRSP 78, 87, 89
conditionality, donors 23–5, 29
consultation 26–7, 45–6
Country Policy and Institutional Assessment
   (CPIA) 107
country-assistance strategies (CAS),
   Bangladesh 102–4
CPESD *see* Co-ordinated Programme for
   Economic and Social Development
CPIA *see* Country Policy and Institutional
   Assessment

debt 3, 10–11, 36
Department for International Development
   (DFID) 105, 107, 113
design of projects 108–11
development partners
   Bangladesh 100–6
   GPRS 51–7
      accountability 47, 60

health services
  Bangladesh 103, 111-12
  Malawi 76, 81-3, 88
heavily indebted poor country (HIPC) debt
  relief 3, 10-11, 35
HIV/AIDS 42-3, 77-8
HPSP see Health and Population Sector
  Programme

IDA see International Development
  Association
IFIs see international financial institutions
IMF see International Monetary Fund
Independent Monitoring Group (IMG)
  13-14, 31, 119-23
individual project support, GPRS 54-5
inflation rates 72
innovation 96
Institute of Statistical, Social and Economic
  Research (ISSER) 44
interest rates 48
International Development Association
  (IDA) 107
international financial institutions (IFIs) 1
  GPRS 33-63
  MPRSP 65-90
  Tanzania 9-32
International Monetary Fund (IMF) 1, 3-4
  approval processes 29
  Bangladesh 91-2, 94-7
  GPRS 37, 46, 52-4, 61
  JSAs 22-3
  letters of intent 4, 23-5
  Tanzania 22-5, 29
irrigation, Ghana 43
ISSER (Institute of Statistical, Social and
  Economic Research) 44

Joint Staff Assessments (JSAs) 22-3, 29

knowledge, local 110-14

legislation in Malawi 80
letters of intent, IMF 4, 23-5
LGRP see Local Government Reform
  Programme
loans, IDA 107
local governance 104
Local Government Reform Programme
  (LGRP), Tanzania 11
local knowledge 110-14

Mahmud, Wahiduddin 91-115
Malawi Economic Growth Strategy (MEGS)
  73-4, 76-7, 86
Malawi Growth and Development Strategy
  (MGDS) 73-4, 76-86, 88-9
Malawi Poverty Reduction Strategy Paper
  (MPRSP) 1-4, 65-90
  annual progress reports 70-1
  budgeting/planning 69-70
  chronology of process 69
  development partner support 81-5
  evolution of process 65-74
  findings/recommendations 85-90
  implementation 70-1, 75-80, 85-9
  lessons learnt 89-90
  outcomes 71-3
  pillars of strategy 67
  planning/budgeting 69-70
  poverty causes/strategies 68
  preparation/content 66-9
  process chronology 69
  quality of strategy 75-80
  recommendations 85-90
  sharing of resources 2002-5 71
  successes/failures 85-8
  weaknesses 77-8, 86-7
MCC see Millennium Challenge Corporation
MDBS see Multi-Donor Budget Support
  programme
MDGs see Millennium Development Goals
Medium-Term Budget Framework (MTBF),
  Bangladesh 98-9
medium-term expenditure frameworks
  (MTEFs)
  GPRS 38, 49-51, 59
  MPRSP 69-70, 79, 87
  Tanzania 12, 21
medium-term priorities/programme (MTPs),
  Ghana 35, 38-9, 49-50
MEGS see Malawi Economic Growth
  Strategy
MEPD see Ministry of Economic Planning
  and Development
MGDS see Malawi Growth and
  Development Strategy
micro-credit 114
micro-enterprise 105
Millennium Challenge Corporation (MCC)
  54-5
Millennium Development Goals (MDGs)
  Bangladesh 100, 106